Step-by-Step Professional Development in Technology

Sarah T. Meltzer, Ed.D.

Eye On Education
6 Depot Way West, Suite 106
Larchmont, NY 10538
(914) 833-0551
(914) 833-0761 fax
www.eyeoneducation.com

For information about permission to reproduce selections from this book, write: Eye On Education, Permissions Dept., Suite 106, 6 Depot Way West, Larchmont, NY 10538

Library of Congress Cataloging-in-Publication Data

Meltzer, Sarah T.
Step-by-step professional development in technology / Sarah T. Meltzer.
        p.   cm.
Includes bibliographical references.
ISBN 978-1-59667-198-0
1. Educational technology—Planning.
2. Computer-assisted instruction—Planning.
I. Title.
LB1028.3.M458 2011
371.33—dc23   2011026840
10 9 8 7 6 5 4 3 2 1

Sponsoring Editor: Robert Sickles
Production Editor: Lauren Davis
Copyeditor: Melissa McDaniel
Designer and Compositor: Matthew Williams, click! Publishing Services
Cover Designer: Dave Strauss, 3FoldDesign

Also Available from EYE ON EDUCATION

About the Author

Sarah T. Meltzer, Ed.D., received her first bachelors degree from Wittenberg University and continued her education with a bachelors, a masters, and a doctorate from Florida Atlantic University. She holds a Florida teaching license in grades one through twelve with a concentration in science and biology. Sarah's interest in technology began as a classroom teacher experimenting with the integration of technology in curriculum through early software activities such as desktop publishing and simple spreadsheets. As a school district instructional technology support teacher, she was able to work with teachers across the district. She then began working as a project manager and educational consultant for Riverdeep Interactive Learning (now Houghton Mifflin Harcourt). With this experience, she was able to work with not only teachers, but also principals and superintendents around the country, to assist them with improving their technology plans to include effective professional development.

Today Sarah is an assistant professor at Western Carolina University and works with pre-service teachers. In addition, she is an educational consultant and assists principals and school district administrators with developing and implementing professional development.

Sarah lives in the mountains of western North Carolina with her husband, dog, and three cats. She enjoys hiking, reading, sewing, and quilting.

meltzerst@aol.com

Acknowledgments

I would like to acknowledge the support of my family who provided unending encouragement and patience in helping me bring this book together. While they are not educators by profession, they have embraced my passion. In addition, I want to thank my colleagues, peers, and students who provided the opportunity and experience that helped me better understand the big picture of education and how human nature affects it. I appreciate their support and understanding.

Table of Contents

About the Author iv

1 Introduction 1
  Why Now? 2
  Purpose of This Book 4

2 Guidelines, Standards, and Recommendations 7
  Current Demand 8
  Gathering Support 9

3 The Big Picture: Preparing for Success 13
  Who? 13
  What? 14
  How? 14
    Goals 14
    Learning Community 15
    Flexibility 16
    Sustainable 16
  Audience = Adult Learners 17
    Motivation 17
    Environment 17
    Interaction 18
  Assessing Needs 18
    Pre-Planning Worksheet Sample 1 19
    Pre-Planning Worksheet Sample 2 20
  Chapter Summary—Checklist 21
  Sample Worksheets/Templates/Guides 22
    Pre-Planning Worksheet 23
    Pre-Planning Worksheet Sample 1 25
    Pre-Planning Worksheet Sample 2 27
    Needs Assessment Survey 29

4 Planning: Setting the Stage 31
  Who Should Be Involved? 32
  Planning Committee (Team) 33
  Setting Goals 34

Developing a Technology Plan. 36
    Long-Term Plan and Short-Term Plan Sample 1 37
    Long-Term Plan and Short-Term Plan Sample 2 38
Chapter Summary—Checklist 39
Sample Worksheets/Templates/Guides 40
    Technology Plan Guide 41
    Technology Inventory 43
    Long-Term Technology Plan Template 44
    Long-Term Technology Plan Sample 1 45
    Long-Term Technology Plan Sample 2 46
    Short-Term Technology Plan Template 47
    Short-Term Technology Plan Sample 1 50
    Short-Term Technology Plan Sample 2 53

5 Implementation: The Action 57
Collaboration 58
Scheduling 59
Training Process 60
    Hands-On Training 61
    Time 61
    Individual Differences 62
    Access 62
    Location 63
    Modeling 63
Support/Resources 63
Evaluation 64
Chapter Summary—Checklist 65
Sample Worksheets/Templates/Guides 66
    Training Schedule Overview 67
    Training Schedule A Sample 68
    Training Schedule B Sample 69

6 Follow-Up and Support: Now What? 71
Support/Resource Person 72
Incentives 73
Ongoing Support 74
Materials and Resources 75
Periodic Review 75
Self-Assessment and Reflection 76
Shared Successes 76
Chapter Summary—Checklist 77
Sample Worksheets/Templates/Guides 78
    Follow-Up Needs Assessment Survey 79

7 Conclusion: Growing the Process 81

Appendix A: References and Resources 85
References 85
Resources.. 86
    Professional and Government Organizations 86
    Hardware and Software Resources...................................... 86

Appendix B: Worksheets/Templates/Guides 88
Pre-Planning Worksheet (Chapter 3). 89
Needs Assessment Survey (Chapter 3).. 91
Technology Plan Guide (Chapter 4) 93
Technology Inventory (Chapter 4)... 95
Long-Term Technology Plan Template (Chapter 4) 96
Short-Term Technology Plan Template (Chapter 4) 97
Training Schedule Overview (Chapter 5)..................................... 100
Training Schedule A Template (Chapter 5). 101
Training Schedule B Template (Chapter 5). 102
Follow-Up Needs Assessment Survey (Chapter 6)............................. 103

Free Downloads

Some of the templates and forms discussed and displayed in this book are also available on Eye On Education's Web site as Adobe Acrobat files. Permission has been granted to purchasers of this book to download these resources and print them.

You can access these downloads by visiting Eye On Education's Web site: **www.eyeoneducation.com**. Click FREE DOWNLOADS or search or browse our Web site to find this book, and then scroll down for downloading instructions.

You'll need your book buyer access code: **PDT-7198-0**

Index of Downloads

Pre-Planning Worksheet 90
Needs Assessment Survey 92
Technology Plan Guide 94
Technology Inventory 96
Long-Term Technology Plan Template 97
Short-Term Technology Plan Template 98
Training Schedule Overview 101
Training Schedule A Template 102
Training Schedule B Template 103
Follow-Up Needs Assessment Survey 104

1 Introduction

This is an exciting and rewarding time to be a part of the educational movement. If you are a positive person who embraces change and challenges as I do, you will agree. If you don't agree, you may have many unresolved concerns regarding education or be a skeptic at heart. Either way, do not stop reading—give me a chance to help make change palatable and worth the effort. This book is not written to convince the reader that professional development in technology is a must or to tell you exactly how to make it happen. Instead, it is written to provide you with research and experience-based approaches to developing and implementing professional development in technology as you address reform in your school. A step-by-step format has been designed to help those charged with leading a school district, individual school, or team of faculty to develop and implement an effective and sustainable professional development plan.

After reviewing and reflecting on the history of education, I believe there have been more positive changes in the past twenty years than in the previous one hundred. Schools are continuously changing and moving forward as they both respond to populations struggling for equality and recognize the importance of diversity for both students and teachers. With the rapid evolution of the American family and a more technology-based workplace, schools are being targeted and challenged to respond.

Transforming schools into exciting and motivating arenas for student learning does not happen overnight, and this transformation cannot be orchestrated by a single person or a small group of creative people in a school. Change is often received as a threat rather than as positive forward movement. In order to meet the modern expectations of the public as well as federal and state requirements, teachers need to improve and, in some cases, adapt their skills and knowledge. This can only be accomplished through effective and sustainable professional development. Teachers who implement changes based on research are more likely to reform their classroom instruction and provide students with the skills necessary to be successful in today's ever-changing world. What was once good enough for grandma, or even mom and dad, is not good enough for our children.

As more and more schools consider reform, apply for grants, and struggle to meet expectations by providing professional development for their faculty and staff, they rely on the same principles they have used in previous initiatives, workshops, and trainings. If you have ever attended a faculty meeting when a principal announced that a technology workshop had been scheduled and everyone was required to attend, you probably saw a mixed response from the teachers. A few faces lit with the excitement of learning new techniques or software. A few faculty quickly looked over their calendars to make sure they had other commitments on that day. Many rolled their eyes and mumbled "here we go again." This last response is not surprising since the majority of school-based technology workshops have been unsuccessful in terms of sustainable impact on classroom instruction and student learning. The terms *professional development*, *workshop*, and *training* are often considered synonymous with *boring*, *same old thing*, and *waste of time*.

My educational experience has taken me from classroom teacher to school district technology support person, project manager, and educational consultant. All of these roles have provided opportunities to work with faculty, staff, administrators, district supervisors, and superintendents as they organized and provided professional development in technology for a variety of needed skills. As project manager, my first step was usually meeting with the principal or designee assigned to coordinate the project. The coordinator was sometimes excited about the upcoming activities. More often, however, coordinators were disinterested or had feelings of both trepidation and concern about the project's success. Those who have been charged with coordinating professional development tend to either follow the same plans they have used in the past or ask the people providing the trainings to do whatever they usually do. For example, as a project manager, I had a principal explain to me that she was not very comfortable with technology and did not understand how teaching her faculty to use computers or software in the classroom would have any influence on student learning. Since the school district required her to provide teacher training in technology, she wanted me to implement one day of training for all teachers, which would be scheduled on a teacher planning day. It is not surprising teachers are often resistant to scheduled trainings that they are required to attend. Often the trainings appear disconnected from their current classroom agendas. Teachers are also resistant because they feel they need the planning day to complete grading and other projects.

Being "asked" by a superintendent or principal to coordinate professional development can be overwhelming even for those with experience. While one individual is usually designated the "responsible" person, he or she should not have to do all the work or "assign" tasks to others. The following chapters are intended to help coordinators and directors look more closely at professional development and approach the process in a more focused and collaborative way.

Why Now?

One of the buzzword phrases of the past ten years is *twenty-first-century skills*. With the lightning advances in technology in recent years, expectations for graduates entering the job market have changed considerably. Consequently, teacher expectations have also risen. The Partnership for 21st Century Skills (2009), an organization supported by the U.S. government, has been one of the leaders in developing and promoting a vision for meeting the educational needs of this century. The organization published the "Framework for 21st Century Learning," which identifies four areas of skills, knowledge, and expertise that students need to master to succeed in today's world. In addition, it includes a support system that helps build a foundation for students to become more engaged in the learning process. A key element of this foundation is professional development.

In support of this trend, in 2010 the U.S. Department of Education released the National Education Technology Plan, titled "Transforming American Education Learning Powered by Technology," which includes a model for technology-supported learning, resources and tools. Such buzzwords, guidelines, and suggestions are becoming more and more difficult for educators to ignore. Chapter 2 of this book is devoted to a review of specific guidelines, standards, and recommendations for professional development by governmental groups and professional organizations. While this book focuses on the step-by-step process of technology-based professional development, it is important to also understand the needs and underlying principles of these processes.

This approach to professional development is a world away from the textbook and curriculum training of the past. Most people do not have extensive knowledge of technology. Teachers attending a workshop or training on a new curriculum or behavior-management technique begin the day with a strong command of the vocabulary of teaching and dealing with children and considerable classroom experience. This is not the case, however, when beginning a workshop on learning how to use newly purchased software or how to integrate computers into the classroom. Many teachers do not have the knowledge base.

School and school district administrators have been providing workshops to train teachers in new curriculum strategies, policies, school procedures, and textbook materials for more than thirty years. When these same processes are used to train teachers in employing technology, the end result is often frustration, negative attitudes, and a sentiment of "this too shall pass." After working with hundreds of schools and school districts attempting to introduce technology into their curriculums, it became clear to me that school administrators and staff flounder as they search for new and successful methods to train and support their teachers, as well as ways to convince faculty and staff that technology is a permanent part of the future. While the preferred implementation of a new basal reading textbook or new math problem-solving strategies may be effectively explained to faculty in a three-hour workshop, the same implementation for technology is not sustainable. Teachers generally come to a workshop with a well-developed foundation for using textbooks and basic teaching strategies. They are open and eager to build on their knowledge. However, when it comes to technology, teachers often lack comfort with the basics of using computers, software, or even digital cameras. In addition, as a group they demonstrate a wide variety of abilities and skill levels. Providing effective and sustainable professional development in technology to a group of teachers requires a very different approach.

While many professional organizations and government education committees have provided support for staff development focused on the use of technology in the classroom, they rarely address the process. It is nearly impossible to find a complete list of procedures to help administrators ensure their activities are worth their efforts. Most agree it is critical for teachers to receive some type of training. While some organizations suggest there are critical steps, it is difficult for administrators to connect all the pieces and develop a solid, effective technology plan. Too often, teacher training becomes a separate entity from the original plan or goal, assuming a goal has actually been predetermined.

Purpose of This Book

This book focuses specifically on the process of how to plan, implement, and manage the professional development of teachers in instructional technology. For the purposes of this book, *instructional technology* is primarily defined as the use of computers or related technology hardware and/or software used to support or enhance the normal instructional process. The term *professional development* is used interchangeably with the terms *training, in-service,* and *staff development.* The processes addressed in this book refer to a group of professional educators working together to learn a new hardware, software, curriculum, or strategy to support the efforts of using technology as part of the normal curriculum. This book is not intended to address the need for teaching technology or to help computer-based teachers improve their technical skills, nor does it address how teachers should instruct students in the use of technology. Rather, it is intended to support administrators, school district personnel, faculty, and staff members by providing clear guidelines and necessary steps to help ensure effective and sustainable professional development. The focus of the professional development may be simply introducing teachers to a newly purchased computer for research in the media center or it may be long-term, such as training and supporting teachers to integrate existing technology into their classroom instruction. In some instances, it may be necessary to convince teachers and staff of the importance of specific professional development. While Chapter 2 provides concrete research to support the need for improving technology skills and supporting teachers in the integration of technology skills in their classroom instruction, this book is not devoted to convincing the reader this topic is important. The importance of providing professional development is addressed to give those developing their own plans important background information they may need to provide to others. Each step in the process in Chapters 3 through 6 is aligned with the supporting need to learn these skills. In essence, this is a step-by-step manual for successful project management of professional development in technology. This process takes into account the big picture, or whole puzzle, as well as the smaller pieces that make up the puzzle to provide sustainability. The extent of the goal will determine the duration of the process.

After researching and analyzing recommended practices and commonly reported best practices by schools, I have compiled the key processes into a step-by-step format to help schools and school districts provide effective and sustainable professional development in technology. *Effective* professional development is "that which results in improvements in teachers' knowledge and instructional practice, as well as improved student learning outcomes" (Darling-Hammond, Jaquith, Mindich, Wei, 2010, p.2). For the purposes of this book, *effective* means that teachers or key participants are using what they learned one year later. The level of success will be related to whether the professional development is sustainable, or in other words, continues to be evident over a long period of time.

In addition, depending on the goal of the professional development, *effective* may relate to meeting the long-term goal, or more importantly, increasing student achievement and supporting reform within the school or district.

This book breaks down the process of providing effective and sustainable professional development from planning through implementation and support. Technology, such as computers provided for teachers in classrooms, should be used as they are intended rather than as dust catchers or bookends. My visits to classrooms months after a teacher training often reveal a computer center littered with dust, papers, and "out of order" signs on computers. A key outcome for sustainable professional development should be a positive impact on student achievement. Research links these and supports the importance of "designing and implementing programs that make a difference in the lives of students" (Joyce, 2002, p.10). Technology sitting idle on tables and stored in closets is not helping instruction.

Although the need to develop and implement an effective and sustainable professional development project is evident to many people, others may need more convincing in the form of research-based data. As the need for school reform and instructional change become more pressing, hopefully, the need to vary and improve classroom instruction will follow. Administrators and faculty alike should embrace the integration of technology in order to meet the needs of children in the twenty-first century. If the information and support provided in Chapter 2 is insufficient, a wealth of information is available on the Internet to help support school administrators connect the steps of the process as they tackle school reform.

Chapters 3 and 4 include two sample technology plans developed for two very different schools. They have been included to give the reader ideas and to clarify the definition of direction. Some discussions of the plans are shared to help readers understand why specific steps were included. However, it is important to review these simply as samples to clarify the process and not to use them as all-inclusive plans. Each plan for professional development should address the unique needs of the students, faculty, and staff. Whether the need is only for a small group of faculty, one grade level, or one small group of targeted students, all the step-by-step processes should be considered. Use these sample plans and suggestions as guidelines and a foundation for discussion within your planning teams.

Chapters 3, 4, and 5 end with a summary checklist. This is intended as a quick reference for readers to review and determine if they have missed any critical pieces. In addition, the worksheets, templates, samples, and guides are listed at the end of each chapter in which they are explained. All of these forms are provided at the end of the book in Appendix B. This format is intended to make them available for easy reference whether they are needed within the text or as a reference at the end. A limited number of common resources are provided at the end of the book as well. They are intended as only a starting point for your resources and not as an endorsement. Because Internet addresses and online resources change frequently, I have provided only a few major Web sites. I encourage readers to use these as a base and to build their own list of links and share current resources. I teach my students to do this by using Microsoft Excel to create a spreadsheet of resources that can be sorted by curriculum topic and type of resource. I wish I had taken my own advice and started this long ago.

2 Guidelines, Standards, and Recommendations

Professional development in technology should be considered a high priority for most schools across the nation. Not only is the fast pace of emerging technologies almost impossible to keep up with, but it is a daunting task simply to support others in becoming comfortable with what might be considered the bare necessities of educational technology. Fortunately, many school districts have been proactive by allowing textbook funds to be used for software purchases or other allocated dollars to be directed toward the purchase of additional computers, digital cameras, document cameras, computer projection equipment, and so on. However, it goes without saying that many of these purchases will remain unused or at least not used to their fullest potential without training and support. Sometimes, school principals are pressured into spending funds at the end of a fiscal year and have little time to research the needs of the faculty or students. In some cases, one or two faculty members may be consulted and purchases will be made based on specific interests and needs. However, if training or support are not considered and the interested faculty members leave the school, those purchases may remain stored in a closet or be rarely used. I have assisted multiple schools with inventories and discovered unopened boxes of software in closets. In some cases, the software was too old to operate on the school's new computers. This is very unfortunate when funds and resources are so limited. Unwise purchases can easily happen when only one or two people have a vision of how particular items, such as digital cameras or specific software, may be used to support a project. Wiser purchases are made when a vision is part of a bigger identified goal. and faculty share ideas and support. Schools need to approach professional development as an opportunity to get the most "bang for their buck," so to speak, with limited funds.

Instructing people in how to use new software and hardware may seem obvious to most. However, at the risk of being redundant, it is important to emphasize that supporting faculty and staff in the use of technology is very different from introducing a new math manipulative to the resource closet or adopting a new basal reader to the third-grade reading program. Unfortunately, there are still numerous teachers who believe if they ignore technology, it will go away. One teacher told me she would definitely retire before computers arrived in *her* classroom. These are the people who need to be convinced, motivated, and encouraged. This particular teacher eventually became motivated after attending multiple workshops and receiving support. She became convinced that computers in her classroom would help her both motivate her students and make her job a little easier. These revelations came to her as her confidence level rose and she realized the benefit of technology in the classroom. I commend her for her perseverance in an area in which she was uncomfortable, and I appreciate the insight she provided me into resistant teachers.

This chapter provides a foundation explaining why professional development in technology is so necessary and fundamentally different from trainings or workshops addressing other kinds of implementations, such as textbooks or reading programs. Some faculty and staff will be eager to learn how to use new technologies or methods to engage their students. Others, however, may need more encouragement and will need to be presented with more concrete reasons. This chapter may help administrators and technology coordinators motivate the more resistant faculty and staff.

Current Demand

Often, it seems technology is everywhere we turn, from the grocery store to the voting booth to the gas station. However, it is still common for teachers to insist they cannot include the Internet or integrate technology into their lesson assignments because many households cannot afford computers or Internet access. While this is sometimes true, recent data indicates this is not as widespread as many may think—or would like—so they can't use it as an excuse. The Pew Internet & American Life Project Survey (2008) revealed that 58 percent of families own two or more computers of which 63 percent are networked. Of these families, 84 percent of the children seven to seventeen years old use the Internet. While 89 percent of families own multiple cell phones, children were found to be less likely to use cell phones than to use the Internet. These numbers are rising more rapidly than the statisticians can collect the data. Not only is technology in various forms more available than ever, but children are often more motivated to use it than to open a textbook.

Schools are attempting to keep up with the demand for technology. The National Center for Educational Statistics (NCES) reported in their report *Teachers' Use of Educational Technology in U.S. Public Schools* (Gray & Lewis, 2010) that 97 percent of teachers have one or more computers in their classrooms. During instructional time, 40 percent of students reportedly used these computers often, and 29 percent reportedly used them sometimes. Between 23 percent and 72 percent of teachers reported having easy access to various instructional technology devices such as digital or liquid projectors (48 percent), interactive whiteboards (28 percent), and digital cameras (64 percent). The percentage of teachers using these devices was reported as 72 percent, 57 percent, and 49 percent respectively. Therefore, the availability of technology in schools for teachers as well as students is not as significant as some might believe.

School districts have been able to make great strides in recent years in acquiring, installing, and maintaining current technology in schools. However, just because most classrooms have computers does not mean that teachers and students are using them for meaningful instructional purposes. Indeed, the National Staff Development Council (NSDC, 2009) reported that teachers were using school computers for five major tasks: administrative processes (76 percent), monitoring student progress (41 percent), research and information (37 percent), instructing students (32 percent), and planning instruction (29 percent). The percentage of computer use directly influencing student achievement is relatively low. It has proven to be difficult to collect data regarding the direct influence of computers on student achievement as technology is generally used as a tool to support and enhance instruction—as it should be. Unfortunately, naysayers have used this fact to point out that technology does not always improve instruction.

Enabling educators to provide the kinds of teaching that will substantially impact student learning and provide school reform requires a much more effective professional development plan than has taken place in the past. If teachers are not provided with training opportunities and have not observed other teachers using technology successfully, they are not likely to understand how it can help them or benefit students. If a person has little background knowledge in a subject, it is understandable that they will not necessarily believe the subject is important. It stands to reason that teachers who are not comfortable using a computer or even an overhead projector will not be motivated to find opportunities to use them during classroom instruction. The *Schools and Staffing Survey* (NSDC, 2009) reported that in 2003–2004 only 14 percent of teachers indicated they believed professional development in using technology in the classroom was important. However, by 2009, 61 percent of teachers believed professional development activities prepared them to use educational technology for instruction (National Center for Educational Statistics, 2009). Progress is being made as multiple professional organizations (such as the National Education Association and the National Staff Development Council) focus on the importance of providing quality learning opportunities for teachers. Hopefully, teachers will take advantage of opportunities if they believe it will benefit instruction.

The U.S. Department of Education has embraced professional development in technology. This is reflected by its release of a draft of the National Educational Technology Plan (2010), which agrees with the view that teachers are not well prepared to use technology for instruction in the classroom.

Gathering Support

While the need for quality training and support to help teachers transform classrooms into effective learning centers is undisputed, the guidelines and recommendations to support this are somewhat limited. The NSDC [recently renamed Learning Forward] provides standards and recommendations for planning and implementing professional development plans for both schools and districts (Roy, 2010). Their most recent release of *Standards for Professional Learning* (2011) indicates "characteristics of professional learning that lead to effective teaching practices, supportive leadership, and improved student results." The largest nonprofit professional organization, the International Society for Technology in Education (ISTE), developed and published National Educational Technology Standards for Teachers in 2008. Many other professional organizations, prominent authors in recognized journals, school districts, and school-based personnel reporting their best practices have provided recommended strategies, guidelines, and characteristic behaviors to assist those planning effective professional development. However, clear comprehensive step-by-step elements of an effective process are not available.

After extensive research of published recommendations, guidelines, and reported suggestions for effective professional development, my findings were compiled and analyzed for commonalities (Meltzer, 2006). While the individual resources provided excellent strategies and suggestions for effective professional development, none included all of the total process needed. Thus, the analysis was extended to include survey responses from principals and teachers who had participated in at least one professional development workshop regarding the use of computer software for instruction. This data was compared with research to develop a better understanding of all steps necessary to plan, implement, and support a sustainable plan for teaching school faculty and staff to integrate technology into their instruction.

This study (Meltzer, 2006) became the foundation for a Model of Effective Professional Development in Technology (Figure 2.1, page 11). The following chapters use this model as a basis for the development of a user-friendly, step-by-step process to serve as a guide for superintendents, principals, teachers, paraprofessionals, technology coordinators, or anyone else charged with the task of providing professional development for faculty or staff. This model is a graphic organizer that shows the key elements and how they fit together as pieces of the puzzle. Looking at the big picture, the process is divided into three basic categories or steps: planning, implementation, and follow-up/support. The key elements fall within these categories, while the resources and support of appropriate administration and faculty are a part of the entire process. Some elements may be customized to fit the specific needs and goals of the technology plan. However, it is important to include all the elements and consider the impact of their interactions. These elements and processes are described in detail in later chapters.

The impact of the professional development should be the focus of the plan as it is developed during the planning step. The long-term goal should directly address specific outcomes such as standards, guidelines, or twenty-first-century skills identified and supported by research. Subsequent chapters address the "how," but first the "what" and "why" must be identified. When the goal is determined, the impact of the success of the goal should be measurable and clear.

School reform today is almost always wrapped around twenty-first-century student outcomes, whether the activities are funded by local districts or grant dollars. As mentioned in the previous chapter, the Partnership for 21st Century Skills (2009) developed their vision in the form of a framework of what students must master to be successful and what support systems should be in place to ensure their success. While these various student outcomes should be interconnected in the learning process, they are specifically identified as:

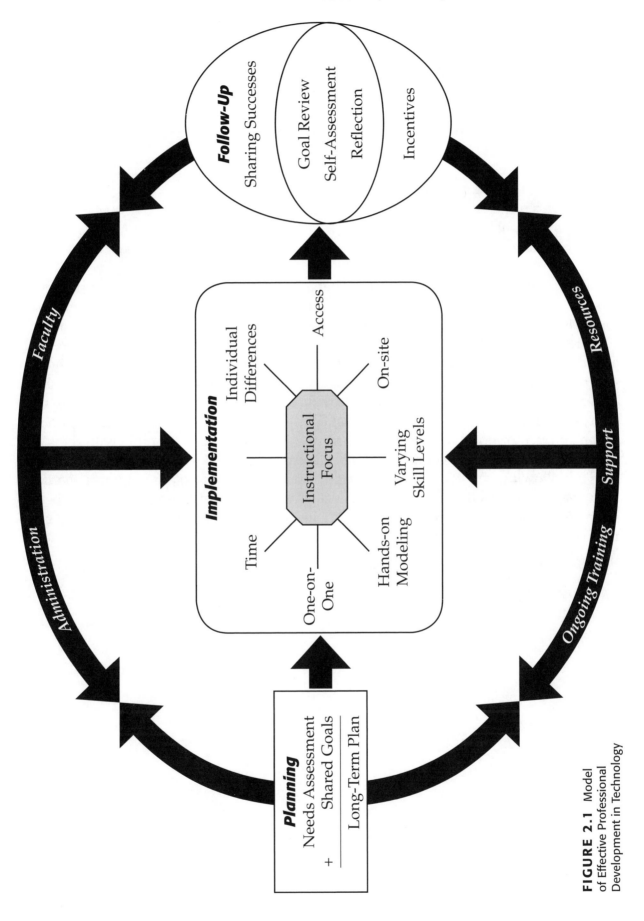

Follow-Up
Sharing Successes
Goal Review
Self-Assessment
Reflection
Incentives

Faculty

Resources

Implementation
Individual Differences
Access
On-site
Instructional Focus
Varying Skill Levels
Time
Hands-on Modeling
One-on-One

Administration

Support

Ongoing Training

Planning
Needs Assessment
+ Shared Goals
Long-Term Plan

FIGURE 2.1 Model of Effective Professional Development in Technology

- ◆ Core subjects and twenty-first-century themes
- ◆ Learning and innovation skills
- ◆ Information, media, and technology skills
- ◆ Life and career skills

The critical support systems necessary for students to master these outcomes are identified as:

- ◆ Standards and assessment
- ◆ Curriculum and instruction
- ◆ Professional development
- ◆ Learning environments

The partnership recommends many behavioral objectives to describe and provide a better understanding of twenty-first-century professional development and learning environments. These should be considered in determining the goal, the impact of a completed goal, and the steps needed to build a strong foundation. For example, a goal addressing an increase in student skills in a core subject such as math using technology will require professional development for teachers. The activities used to accomplish the goal must be based on standards and provide a positive learning environment to support the foundation for meeting this goal. Without a strong foundation, any successes will be limited or not sustainable. Compare the elements in this example with the list of outcomes above, and the connection will be a little clearer.

The following chapters provide a step-by-step process for planning, implementing, and supporting effective professional development. Many of these steps are aligned to the recommended student outcomes and to the goal of establishing model learning environments to provide a strong foundation. In addition, the samples provided include the necessary connection to these guidelines.

3 The Big Picture: Preparing for Success

The Model of Effective Professional Development (Figure 2.1, page 11) shows five puzzle pieces interacting with each other. The three main pieces, or steps, are planning, implementation, and follow-up. They are sequential, and each includes specific elements that may be customized and molded to support the goal or focus of the overall technology plan. For example, the Implementation piece must have an instructional or student achievement focus. While all the surrounding elements in that piece need to be considered, each may have a different priority or weight within the implementation process. The top and bottom pieces act as insulation and should interact with all three of the sequential center pieces. The top piece relates to the involvement of administration and faculty throughout the project. The bottom piece represents not only the existence of resources and support but also the level of interaction of these within each step of the process. These pieces will be addressed in more detail in the following chapters. It may be helpful to refer back to the model following each chapter.

Who?

The first question that comes to mind is who should be responsible. As previously mentioned, the responsibility for professional development in technology varies from school district to school district. Sometimes a principal is assigned the task, and then the principal designates a faculty member or school technology resource person. In many school districts, professional development in technology is the responsibility of the technology coordinator. Regardless of who is made responsible, it is important that the person not believe it is up to him or her to do all of the steps alone. Instead, this person should consider the role to be one of facilitator or motivator. Depending on the size of the plan, it may be that person's responsibility to identify all involved parties and help determine a leadership team. However, it is not the facilitator's role to independently develop the plan or implement all the pieces of the puzzle. Collaboration and involvement of the leadership team and the stakeholders is the key. This will become clearer as the steps and processes are defined.

What?

Getting started is definitely one of the most difficult steps of any project and probably accounts for more project failures than any other step. This need not be the case if several key elements are taken into account. Specifically, as the professional development plan evolves, the following basic elements should be imbedded in the process:

◆ Focus on a specific learning goal and/or student outcome.
◆ Build a learning community through collaboration.
◆ Be flexible and supportive of learning styles and needs.
◆ Provide a sustainable structure for support and continued learning.

These four elements are the basic building blocks for the foundation of an effective professional development plan and will be more fully developed in subsequent chapters.

How?

The following overview of how to build this foundation will provide a better understanding.

Goals

The learning goal(s) should be directly related to measurable student achievement, which can be enhanced by developing the faculty's skills and understanding. It will be easier to focus on the professional development activities if the goal is clearly defined and agreed upon by all the stakeholders. More often than not, this goal can be easily defined based on data-driven results of high-stakes testing and school curriculum reviews. Developing your goals based on these elements will often open doors to available funding and support from grants, state or federal funds, or commercial sources. For example, a school improvement plan may include the goal to improve ninth-grade student algebra skills through the use of specific teaching strategies incorporating the use of interactive white boards in classrooms. Providing faculty and staff with the necessary skills to be able to integrate their lessons with this technology is an example of a very specific data-driven goal. The accomplishment of this goal will provide a substantial support system to ensure students can improve in their core subject area of algebra. In this example, the long-term goal is to improve ninth-grade students' algebra knowledge, and the short-term goal is to improve faculty and staff technology integration skills. Both goals are realistic and measurable.

If the goal targets a limited number of students, it is no less important. For example, the goal may be to improve measurement skills for third-grade at-risk students. While the targeted audience may include only fifteen students, two teachers, and a curriculum resource person, it should be approached with the same attitude. Through collaboration and the building of a strong plan, other goals may become more attainable. Do not underestimate the significance of small steps.

Learning Community

Developing a solid professional learning community (PLC) is an important building block for any future changes. A strong community of learners can only be built through cooperation, open communication, and strong collaboration. Begin by identifying the existing learning communities that exist within the school, such as grade-level or subject-level teams, team leaders, or curriculum support/resource teams. Some of these may be obvious and already identified as existing teams. However, some communities may not be as obvious and may have only a common thread through relationships, interests, or common responsibilities. Do not overlook strong existing frameworks so you are not reinventing the wheel. Build on what you have and expand the community to include any who choose to join. By taking the time to invite anyone to join, it may be possible to increase and overlap smaller learning communities and to include members who are eager to be involved. Although it may take extra effort, time, and patience to communicate the goal and provide opportunities for others to join the community, it is important to be sure all key stakeholders are part of this identified learning community. Beware of relying on preconceived ideas as to who might be included in this group.

I cannot emphasize enough the importance of taking into account *all* the participants who should be involved. For example, if the goal is to improve math skills for a specific group of students, be sure to include any faculty or staff members who may have contact with the targeted students and may be able to offer support or feedback on the project. Do not forget to consider media support staff and resource and instructional support faculty/staff. If any one group of people is ignored or feels thwarted, the members will not only fail to participate, but they may also undermine the process. It is impossible to please everyone; however, it is important to let everyone know an attempt has been made to consider and meet as many needs as possible. While it may seem like too many people may be involved and there are more queen bees than workers, the people who actually come to the meetings to work are very small in number. The positive outcome of this process will be not only to allow all stakeholders an opportunity to be involved and informed but also to build a strong leadership team to support the plan. This leadership team will be the project's motivators and facilitators. In a large school district project, this team may consist of influential faculty, administrators, and district coordinators. However, in a small single-school project it may consist of the principal, a resource teacher, and a faculty member. The goals and expected outcomes should guide the development of the PLC and leadership team.

Spending time on developing a strong PLC and maintaining it throughout the process is well worth the effort. A considerable PLC builds a much stronger foundation for support of the plan and, hence, support for the long-term goal.

Flexibility

When the effort is made to create a diverse and strong PLC, it stands to reason the members will be diverse in their personal goals, schedules, and willingness to be involved. Although it may not always be easy and may take longer than expected, most effective and sustainable professional development plans will be those that are flexible and supportive. It might be helpful to look at the word *flexibility* and use it interchangeably with *options*. By providing options for opportunities, the plan can appear much more flexible. While it may not be perfect for everyone, more will be satisfied with the attempt than if their needs appear to have been ignored. While this may seem like a small compromise, it can have a strong impact on the foundation of the learning community.

In the case of a large project, it may be best to have the leadership team consider the targeted group with the highest need and consider opportunities more conducive to this group. It might also be possible to develop phases of the project addressing opportunities for multiple audiences at a later date. Smaller projects will not be a challenge when it comes to scheduling and being flexible with opportunities.

Sustainable

This is the piece that is often missing when the project activities have been completed and the funds have been spent. A year after the training has been completed the principal or technology coordinator may realize the software has rarely been used in the classroom. After all the time and effort involved in planning, not to mention implementation, there is nothing worse than feeling as though you did not accomplish your goals or that you need to start all over again. To avoid such feelings from the beginning, be sure to include support and additional professional development opportunities to enhance and improve the process. For example, share progress and encourage feedback often through regular meetings, newsletters, social networking, blogs, or even old-fashion bulletin boards and public announcements. Continue to reassess and refine or redefine the original goal as the project moves forward. Most importantly, do not forget to share and communicate the process as it progresses. Be sure all participants know what has taken place and what may have been altered to improve the process. Knowing why steps have been delayed or schedules changed encourages participants to have a positive outlook. For example, if the interactive whiteboards are going to be a month delayed in delivery and installation, the implementation may be delayed from the original plan. In other words, it is better to wait for the hardware rather than continue with training just because it was already scheduled. If this information is shared with participants and they feel they are part of the process and decision making, they generally will be more positive and supportive. Awareness can support sustainability. Sometimes administrators believe faculty members are too busy and do not want to be bothered with details. However, in my experience, people want to know why decisions have been made. This does not mean they want to take an active part in making the decision, but they want to know about it. Maybe this supports why gossip travels faster than knowledge.

Audience = Adult Learners

Educators are sometimes accused of treating everyone around them as students. I have tried to avoid this scenario, especially at home, but my family has found me guilty of this more than a few times. Because all participants involved in professional development of technology fall in the adult learner category, it is important to keep adult learning theories in mind. Adults need to be treated as adults. This important concept should not be disregarded during the professional development process.

There is extensive research on how adult learners are motivated and learn. Andragogy, the study of teaching adults to learn, has been well established over the past thirty years by multiple well-known theorists and researchers (Merriam & Caffarella, 1999; Maurer & Davidson, 1998; Knowles, 1984; Galbraith, Sisco, & Guglielmino, 1997). When considering professional development in technology, much of this research can be divided into three important categories: motivation, environment, and interaction.

Motivation

Adult learners need to be motivated by intrinsic rather than extrinsic rewards. Adults are generally self-directed and need to feel the goal will have a personal effect on them and/or their working environment. Any knowledge learned must be transferable to the classroom and, ideally, help teachers feel directly responsible for their own success in helping students achieve. Extrinsic rewards such as money, hardware, and extra time can be beneficial for the improvement of attendance for professional development events. However, their effects have a much shorter duration. They do not last much longer than the event and presentation of the reward. Adult learners who believe the activity will provide valuable personal knowledge will attend regardless of the material rewards; however, extrinsic rewards will put smiles on their faces, which adds to a positive environment. Rewards can be creative and do not have to expensive. It is often surprising what will motivate people, so do not underestimate them. I am always surprised that many high school students are motivated by stickers, and college students are often motivated by ice cream parties. It is often the presentation and approach that helps instill the motivation.

Environment

The location, agenda, and materials for adult learners must be well planned, clearly focused on the goals, time efficient, and sensitive to the participants. Communication of the attempt to consider the comforts and learning styles of all participants will help provide a good adult learning environment. Multiple opportunities to learn and participate will increase the success of the professional development. Adults need to feel they are making a good choice by participating and will personally benefit from the experience. Every attempt should be made to consider participants' potentially different learning styles and ability levels. When all teachers and support faculty with different personal goals are required to attend a one-day training, the environment will not necessarily be conducive to learning. Several small focused groups will accomplish more because the participants will have common goals and feel the activities are geared toward their personal interests. The environment must be as positive and supportive as possible. Location can sometimes be a very important factor. If teachers might be distracted by their classroom or student responsibilities, it may be better to provide training away from their home school. Determining the most conducive learning environment must take in to account the needs, personalities, and logistics of the faculty and school as well as what options are available. If there are no alternative locations, consider all the other factors regarding the organization, materials, and comfort of the learning environment. It is not always about location.

Interaction

Because adults need to be able to connect what they are learning with what they already know, total involvement and integrated activities with their peers help to reinforce any new knowledge and the need to implement new skills. While some adults prefer to learn independently, most can learn well working in groups with respected peers. Many have not had this opportunity or have had little experience with collaboration, so they may be apprehensive. A positive approach can help faculty experience the benefits of this type of interaction.

These characteristics of adult learners are important to keep in mind throughout the process. They are key during the planning and implementation phases, while building a learning community, and for the continued support of the plan.

Assessing Needs

The previous sections in this chapter address the human foundation and the development of a strong learning community and leadership team. Collecting concrete information to support the plan can take place simultaneously with the beginning of the project. The development and distribution of a needs assessment survey can be a good area for first discussions. This not only includes everyone but also helps inform faculty and staff of the scope of the project while allowing them to give input. It will help narrow the focus of what needs to be done, what goals should be targeted, and where funds may need to be budgeted. More importantly, it may provide insight into attitudes of faculty and staff as well as who might be motivated and willing to be a strong supporter. Sometimes a survey to determine needs will provide surprising results and completely change the original course of a project. Skipping this step or disregarding the results as unimportant may prove to be a mistake in the long run. It needs to be part of the big picture and discussed in the early stages before the actual plan begins. The Needs Assessment Survey (which can be found at the end of this chapter and in Appendix B) is addressed specifically in the next chapter. This survey may also help determine specific learning needs and limitations of the participants. Do not treat these needs lightly.

A Pre-Planning Worksheet (which can be found at the end of this chapter and in Appendix B) may also be helpful in examining the big picture. Sometimes this can help a collaborative group focus more clearly on their goals and needs. The worksheet should be used only as a beginning framework during a brainstorming session. Add and refine areas as they are brought to the attention of the learning community. Consider all suggestions and try to think of it as a wish list. Encourage the group to think outside the box and try not to focus only on what is available. It is easy to say a specific suggestion is impossible because there is not enough time or a specific group of people cannot get together for a workshop because it would not be allowed by administration. Try to guide the brainstorming session so that suggestions will be made without the "we can't do this because" syndrome. By approaching the first phase with this "wish list" attitude, expectations will be higher and participants will be more willing to discuss solutions that may not have been previously explored.

In order to help clarify the use of the Pre-Planning Worksheet, two samples are provided: Pre-Planning Worksheet Sample 1 and Pre-Planning Worksheet Sample 2. These two samples, which represent very different scenarios, should not be considered templates to which you should add or delete information for your own plan. Instead, use the blank worksheets as templates and look at the samples to help clarify and provide ideas. It is important to think about your own school faculty and student needs and be sure all actions are related to these. Use the included samples as guidelines and frames of reference for clarification purposes.

Pre-Planning Worksheet Sample 1

Pre-Planning Worksheet Sample 1 is based on the scenario of an elementary school that found the standardized scores of their students in grades three through five needed improvement to meet the expectations of the school district. A needs assessment survey of the faculty and staff indicated that the technology in the school was not being used effectively. Teachers and staff complained they did not have access to updated classroom technology. Consequently, the administration decided to form a leadership (planning) committee to brainstorm and consider how these needs could be incorporated into a plan to improve the situation. The worksheet was completed using a brainstorming technique as the committee considered all plausible goals and pieces of the plan.

Goals should always be written in such a way that they are observable and measurable. In other words, it is important to be able to determine to what degree the goals are already taking place and to what degree (a measurable amount) they are taking place following the plan. For example, the goal of increasing the use of technology in classroom instruction can be measured now and in the future through the use of a survey from teachers or observations from administration. The goal of increasing standardized test scores is easy to measure, as are the training of teachers and the purchase of hardware. The most powerful or significant goals are those easily aligned with district goals, national guidelines, or twenty-first-century skills. The Pre-Planning Worksheet Sample 1 clearly addresses multiple twenty-first-century goals for students as well as the building of a foundation for success as described at the end of Chapter 2. These are important considerations when applying for grant dollars, whether public or private.

Once the list of goals is completed, the next step is to prioritize the goals and divide them into long-term goals and short-term goals. In Sample 1, the first two goals are long term. The next three goals are short term and are critical steps in building the foundation for the long-term goals. These goals will reappear in samples in later chapters, and it may be helpful to refer back to this planning worksheet as you review them in Chapter 4.

The second section of the worksheet sample considers the learning community, a concept that is often overlooked. Hopefully, there will be members of many of these groups on the leadership committee completing this worksheet. In reviewing the groups on the list, it is important to see that some of the members might overlap. For example, each grade-level team from grade three through five includes a grade chairperson. Each of these grade chairpersons is also a member of the leadership team. The leadership team also includes a representative of special education teachers and resource teachers. By considering all the various groups within the school, formal or informal, no interested faculty or staff will be excluded.

The next sections of the worksheet include a variety of locations and times for professional development trainings. These are listed as part of the brainstorming activity and should not be used as specific training plans. More detailed schedules and plans come later as the process evolves. However, schedules are generally on the minds of most people as soon as the first meetings begin. It is better to include them in a general sense in order to focus more on the goals and how they will be determined.

Pre-Planning Worksheet Sample 2

Pre-Planning Worksheet Sample 2 represents the results of a leadership committee meeting in a high school. The school administration received student math scores that were below average for the school district. A survey of teachers and students within the school also indicated low motivation for at-risk ninth-grade students and the teachers working with these students. The school administration decided to develop a comprehensive plan to help address these needs. At this point in the process, it is important to prioritize and categorize the goals according to their importance and what needs to be done first in order to build a foundation to accomplish the higher goals. In this sample, the first two goals are long-term goals, while the other goals are short term. These secondary goals are important foundation steps in order to ensure the success of the long-term goals.

During pre-planning discussions and after reviewing needs assessment surveys, the leadership committee in Sample 2 determined the addition of instruction-based math software that could be used in the classroom would help meet the needs of diverse learners. This software would provide additional visual and auditory support for instruction and help motivate students to be more interested in math. With effective professional development, the addition of technology into classroom instruction could also help motivate teachers. The key is effective introduction and professional development so teachers do not believe the technology is more work or something extra they need to do.

The sample plan identifies the goal of training teachers working directly with the targeted ninth-grade students. This training is necessary to ensure effective use of the software, and it will provide motivation for teachers working with the at-risk students.

The math teachers will receive software access in their rooms, in computer labs, and online from home as incentives. Also, teachers will be given extra time and opportunities to collaborate on integrated lesson plans to help motivate them to use the software in the classroom. Additional incentives will be addressed in subsequent chapters. Overall, the opportunity for support and resources will motivate teachers and encourage them to work together to meet long-term goals. From this example, it is evident that a strong foundation of short-term goals must be met to ensure the success of the long-term goals.

The purpose of the Pre-Planning Worksheet should be evident from these samples and the discussion above. The conversations necessary to answer the questions should prompt the planning committee to discuss not only the obvious needs of the faculty and students but also the positive resources and learning environment in which the professional development will take place. While each school site includes unique personalities and concerns, these questions and discussions will help faculty and administrators develop a more successful and comprehensive professional development plan. This pre-planning step should concentrate on the big picture as opposed to the details of the goals and activities that will be planned. While it is important to record the goals that emerge from the brainstorming activities, the Pre-Planning Worksheet is not the place to develop the plan in detail. That will be addressed in the following chapter.

The big picture addressed in this chapter considers the foundation for developing an effective and sustainable plan for professional development in technology. The step-by-step process that follows in the next three chapters will evolve easily with these first steps in place. In your review the Model of Effective Professional Development in Technology (Figure 2.1) again, it will be apparent that the steps of planning, implementing, and supporting the professional development are straightforward. As you read through the next three chapters, I encourage you to revisit these basic principles and keep the big picture in focus. Many of the basic elements will be revisited and clarified at the risk of being redundant. However, I believe it is more important to help readers understand the concept than to be afraid of repeating myself. Some of you may want to come back and look at the big picture after you have absorbed the details. I understand and support that approach.

Chapter Summary—Checklist

1. Keep the big picture in mind for success and remember to:
   - ☐ Focus on the goal
   - ☐ Build a learning community
   - ☐ Be flexible and supportive
   - ☐ Provide a sustainable structure
2. Keep adult learner characteristics in mind as you consider:
   - ☐ Motivation
   - ☐ Environment
   - ☐ Interaction

Sample Worksheets/Templates/Guides

- Pre-Planning Worksheet 23
- Pre-Planning Worksheet Sample 1. 25
- Pre-Planning Worksheet Sample 2. 27
- Needs Assessment Survey 29

Pre-Planning Worksheet (Wish List)

I. Goals (List all possible goals regardless of their priority.):

II. Learning community:
   A. Existing learning groups/teams:

   B. Additional learning groups/teams needed (These may overlap and may include others outside the community):

III. Options for meeting/training locations:

IV.   Options for meeting/training times:

V.   Training materials (wish list):

VI.   Resources (wish list):

VII. Assessment/evaluation:

Pre-Planning Worksheet Sample 1

I. Goals (List all possible goals regardless of their priority.):
    - Increase language arts skills for students in grades three to five
    - Increase the use of technology integration into classroom curriculum
    - Increase the level of teacher knowledge/expertise on the use of interactive whiteboards
    - Purchase, install, and implement the use of interactive whiteboards in all grades three through five classrooms
    - Train teachers to use interactive whiteboards

II. Learning community:
    A. Existing learning groups/teams:
        - Grade-level teams
        - Team leaders (leadership team)
        - Special education teachers
        - Resource/support teachers (media, reading resource teacher, speech teacher, computer lab teacher)
        - Parent/teacher organization board members

    B. Additional learning groups/teams needed (These may overlap and may include others outside the community):
        - Vendor and representative (software/hardware/training support)
        - District curriculum specialist (support)
        - District technology (support)
        - Cadre of classroom teachers to assist in support (those with existing knowledge/experience using interactive whiteboards and/or those with a strong interest in joining the support team)

III. Options for meeting/training locations:
    - School computer lab
    - Classroom
    - Media center
    - District office

IV.   Options for meeting/training times:
- *Planning days (noninstructional)*
- *Instructional days during teacher planning periods*
- *Before- and/or after-school hours*
- *Saturdays*
- *Vacation days*

V.   Training materials (wish list):
- *Software/hardware installed and functional in all locations*
- *Curriculum guides*
- *Vendor guides for software/hardware*
- *Sample lessons using software/hardware as models*

VI.   Resources (wish list):
- *Vendor support*
- *School district support for technology and curriculum*
- *Trainer with expertise and knowledge of curriculum*
- *Several lead teachers to model integration of technology*

VII.   Assessment/evaluation:
- *Standardized tests*
- *Survey/feedback from teachers*
- *Survey/feedback from students*
- *Observations from administrators*

Pre-Planning Worksheet Sample 2

I.   Goals (List all possible goals regardless of their priority.):
- Increase math scores for ninth-grade at-risk students
- Increase the use of technology in the classroom by math teachers
- Select, purchase, and install appropriate math software for ninth-grade students
- Provide adequate access to software for all math teachers
- Train teachers to use software

II.   Learning community:
    A. Existing learning groups/teams:
- All math teachers
- Team leaders (from each curriculum area)
- Special education teachers
- Resource/support teachers (media teacher, reading resource teacher, speech teacher, computer lab teacher)
- Parent/teacher organization board members

    B. Additional learning groups/teams needed (These may overlap and may include others outside the community):
- Vendor (software/hardware/training support)
- District curriculum specialist (support)
- District technology (support)
- Cadre of classroom teachers to assist in support or one or two key math teachers to model expectations and support peers

III. Options for meeting/training locations:
- School computer lab
- Resource room with computers
- Media center
- District office

IV. Options for meeting/training times:
- *Planning days (noninstructional)*
- *Instructional days during teacher planning periods*
- *Before- and/or after-school hours*
- *Saturdays*
- *Vacation days*

V. Training materials (wish list):
- *Software installed and functional in all locations needed for math teachers*
- *Curriculum guides aligned to math curriculum*
- *Vendor guides for software*
- *Sample lessons using software*

VI. Resources (wish list):
- *Vendor support*
- *School district support for technology and curriculum*
- *Trainer with expertise and knowledge of curriculum*
- *Several math teachers to model integration of technology (possibly one class-room teacher and one resource teacher)*

VII. Assessment/evaluation:
- *Standardized tests*
- *Classroom assessments*
- *Survey/feedback from teachers*
- *Survey/feedback from students*
- *Observations from administrators*

Needs Assessment Survey (Professional Development)

Consider the information needed to create a quality professional development plan. Faculty and staff must be able to develop a comfort level with the necessary hardware, software, and implementation plan in order to successfully meet the expectation level set for the goals. Modify this needs assessment survey by including questions that will provide appropriate and adequate information needed to create a plan.

Please respond to each question using the following scale:

1 = very uncomfortable, 2 = somewhat uncomfortable,
3 = somewhat comfortable, 4 = very comfortable

1. My comfort level using the following hardware:
   a. Computer ① ② ③ ④
   b. Projector ① ② ③ ④
   c. Interactive whiteboard ① ② ③ ④
   d. Digital camera ① ② ③ ④
   e. Other _____
2. My comfort level using the following type of software:
   a. Word processing ① ② ③ ④
   b. Desktop publishing (i.e. Microsoft Publisher) ① ② ③ ④
   c. Spreadsheet software (i.e. Excel) ① ② ③ ④
   d. Other _____
3. My comfort level using the hardware and/or software integrated into my lesson plans: ① ② ③ ④

Please answer the following questions by selecting YES or NO:

5. I would like to improve my comfort level using the hardware by:
   a. Attending appropriate scheduled training (initial, advanced, etc.) Ⓨ Ⓝ
   b. Receiving a manual or handouts Ⓨ Ⓝ
   c. Observing someone using the hardware Ⓨ Ⓝ
   d. Going to a Web site with training/support information Ⓨ Ⓝ
   e. Other (please describe your preference if not listed) _____
6. I would like to improve my comfort level using the software by:
   a. Attending appropriate scheduled training (initial, advanced, etc.) Ⓨ Ⓝ
   b. Receiving a manual or handouts Ⓨ Ⓝ
   c. Observing someone using the hardware Ⓨ Ⓝ
   d. Going to a Web site with training/support information Ⓨ Ⓝ
   e. Other (please describe your preference if not listed) _____

7. I would like to improve my ability to integrate the software
   into my lesson plans by:
   a. Attending appropriate scheduled training (initial, advanced, etc.) Ⓨ Ⓝ
   b. Receiving a manual or handouts Ⓨ Ⓝ
   c. Observing someone using the hardware Ⓨ Ⓝ
   d. Going to a Web site with training/support information Ⓨ Ⓝ
   e. Other (please describe your preference if not listed) _____
8. I would be willing to:
   a. Share my knowledge with other faculty/staff Ⓨ Ⓝ
   b. Model the software/hardware/lessons in my classroom Ⓨ Ⓝ
   c. Assist with training as a peer or team member Ⓨ Ⓝ
   d. Develop training materials to support colleagues Ⓨ Ⓝ
   e. Other: _____
9. The most important things in my opinion to consider when
   planning professional development are (#1 is the most important):

   1. _____

   2. _____

   3. _____
10. In my opinion, the goal of the professional development should be:

   _____

   _____

4 Planning: Setting the Stage

The planning process is the most important step. This is not to say the processes that follow should be discounted. However, the approach and first steps of the planning stage are critical for establishing a strong sense of purpose and collaboration among the participants. A negative approach can stop any progress before it gets started. If the learning community has been well established as discussed in the preceding chapter, collaboration will come more easily. In fact, if there are opportunities for faculty and staff to share and discuss the activities, goals, and successes, collaboration will take place regularly without effort. This is a sign of a strong professional learning community. You are well on your way to being successful.

The initial decision to plan and implement professional development in technology can come from many sources, such as district mandates, new hardware or software purchases, or new funding. Regardless of what originates this process, it is important to establish clear goals. The most obvious goals will be driven by the purpose of the project. For example, if the district or school has received money designated for professional development and funding to purchase computers or other technology, such as projectors for the schools, the obvious goal is to train teachers to use the new technology. Notably, a longer-term approach is to focus on how teachers skilled in using technology will be more apt to integrate the technology into their classroom instruction. Research indicates students whose teachers use technology show an increase in student achievement, and the ultimate goal is to increase student learning. Therefore, purchasing equipment and training teachers to use the equipment must be coupled with developing a comfort level for teachers to integrate the technology into the learning process. While the short-term plan is to train teachers to use the new technology, the long-term goal should focus on student achievement. A strong, effective plan to meet these goals, both short-term and long-term, will be evident as the stakeholders progress through several critical steps.

The previous chapter discussed the need to complete a pre-planning worksheet in preparation for specific plans. If you have chosen to skip the previous chapter, I encourage you to go back and read it before you proceed. Having meaningful conversations and brainstorming sessions with all the stakeholders not only makes the true planning process easier but also ensures greater success for the overall goals. One major reason for unsuccessful professional development, or "money not spent wisely," is a weak plan. More often than not, a weak plan is one that is not aligned with long-term goals or has goals that are not aligned to standards such as twenty-first-century skills. These plans can be thought of as "a flash in the pan" or "silver-bullet training," where administrators believe that a single training will solve the problem. Then they wonder later why teachers aren't using the software, strategy, or materials. While time is always of the essence and there never seems to be enough of it in a school, it is critical to take the time to develop a solid foundation for any professional development.

Who Should Be Involved?

When the principal or technology director has been given the task of training teachers to use new technology, planning may take different directions. For instance, the principal might pass the task to an assistant principal or technology resource person at the school. Alternatively, this task may fall on the shoulders of a committee of teachers. It does not really matter who takes the reins and acts as the facilitator or leader of the project, as long as that person or committee sets the stage appropriately. This process was addressed in some detail in the previous chapter in the section describing learning communities and developing a leadership team. Who is involved will vary considerably from district to district and school to school.

Regardless of who facilitates the planning, it is important for the principal and other key administrators to be involved and present at initial planning meetings. This does not mean these individuals should dominate the discussions or decisions, and they do not have to attend every activity. In some cases, it may be better if they do not attend all the meetings. However, it is important for the participants to know that the administrators value the project and the outcome. In addition, when administrators are part of this process, they better understand the obstacles and concerns of the teachers involved. In turn, their expectations are more realistic. I have been told by several principals who attended my trainings that they were surprised by comments their teachers made. The principals had not been aware of many of the teachers' concerns and challenges. This knowledge helped the principals eliminate problems before they developed, validated faculty concerns, and motivated faculty involvement. The perception of administrative involvement should be a part of the plan from the beginning.

The first step in making this involvement evident is for the principal or designated coordinator to share with the faculty and staff the goals and primary reasons the professional development is being planned. This informs the stakeholders of the basic goals and of the expectation that the training will take place. Also, this confirms to the faculty that the administration is involved and endorses the project. As mentioned in the last chapter, it is important to include all possible stakeholders and those who may provide support in the initial planning stages. More heads are almost always better than a few. Even a professional development plan initiated top-down by a superintendent can be improved with an approach that uses endorsement through sharing and a sense of involvement.

The planning process does not need to be an all-faculty get-together. Once everyone is invited to participate, those who choose to be involved with the planning should meet. Forcing all faculty members to join could backfire and encourage dissent or a division among the faculty. For example, if the goal is to increase reading skills for third-grade students, it may be important to include all fine arts teachers in the initial discussion. As the planning progresses, a short-term plan may include purchasing e-readers and training teachers to integrate this technology into the classroom. At this point, it would be important to involve media and resource teachers in the planning; however, physical education and music teachers may not be interested. But rather than make some faculty feel they are being excluded or having something irrelevant forced on them, all stakeholders should be kept informed as to the purpose, goals, and progress of the plan. As the process progresses, include those who are willing to be supportive. This also helps the process to become more achievable.

Planning Committee (Leadership Team)

The next step in getting the faculty involved is to establish a planning committee or leadership team, as introduced in the previous chapter. The title of this group is not as important as is its function. The principal should encourage people from all areas of the school that will be influenced by the training to participate. It is important to have all subject areas or grade levels represented. In some cases, it might be necessary for the principal to invite specific people to participate. It is important to have input from as many different viewpoints as possible. The planning committee should have enough members to represent the school well, yet it should be manageable. Sometimes this may take one-on-one encouragement from specific people. It is possible the pre-planning was completed by a small group of people writing a grant for the school or district, or a group of administrators considering budget needs for the school year. Therefore, it may be necessary to back up a step and create a new "expanded" planning committee to include the stakeholders. The reality is that this cannot always be done as the very first step. That does not mean this step should be skipped.

The planning committee should preferably be led by someone other than the principal or someone else with a strong administrative influence. If the principal is the leader, some committee members may feel the planning is administratively driven. It is important for participants to support the goal and to understand that the planning is goal driven.

By demonstrating visible administrative involvement and the willingness to solicit suggestions from all faculty members, the foundation of this stage will be well built. A strong collaborative environment can only be developed when all participants believe they are involved and their concerns are being heard. This is why it is important to go back and include all the stakeholders—or at least encourage them to participate. This planning committee will be the guiding force, the facilitators, and the overseers as the project begins. The committee may ultimately become the leadership committee or a smaller group may evolve from this group to be the team of leaders.

Setting Goals

The basic goal or expectation of the professional development should be general in the beginning and, over time, be fine-tuned or developed in more detail based on the individual expectations and needs of the school, faculty, and students. The term *general* is not to mean "simple"; rather, the goal needs to be at the top of the big picture and should be the priority. This goal or expectation may vary in a multitude of ways. In order to customize it, it is important to obtain a clear picture of the needs and levels of understanding of the expected participants. For example, if the general goal is to train all kindergarten through fifth-grade teachers how to use an interactive whiteboard and integrate it into lessons, all teachers who are expected to attend training and use the technology should provide input as to their expertise and needs. While this is a worthy goal and can be measured, it may be worth looking at it as part of an even bigger picture. A long-term goal may be to improve math skills for all kindergarten through fifth-grade students. Training teachers to use interactive whiteboards for some of their math instruction would be an excellent short-term goal in this case. Both goals in this case are data driven, an important aspect to any goal setting.

Input from faculty and staff can always be obtained through discussions and meetings. However, the most efficient way is through the distribution of a needs assessment survey (see Appendix B) as introduced at the end of the previous chapter. By providing an opportunity for people to reflect on their own personal goals and situations, they will respond more candidly to a written survey. When questions aligned to the goals and activities are asked, it is easier for participants to focus their responses on the areas where input is needed. However, be sure to include an opportunity for open-ended questions to allow for creative responses or concerns the planning committee may not have considered.

The included sample survey is designed to obtain information from faculty or staff regarding their comfort level with the use of technologies and what their perceptions may be regarding training aspects. This sample is provided as a template and should be customized to identify specific areas relating to the goals or expectations of the project. It is virtually impossible to create a survey that would be appropriate for all situations. Additional samples are available on the Internet or from professional organizations. It is important to consider what information the planning committee may need in order to plan effective professional development. By customizing the needs assessment survey, the key information can be obtained in a short form without requiring faculty to complete unnecessary information. The simpler and more concise the survey, the more likely the faculty will be to complete it. It also might be helpful to distribute several short needs assessments over a period of time targeting different aspects of the project. This is especially appropriate if the major goal is long-term but includes many short-term goals.

An easy way to deliver the survey is via e-mail, but with e-mail, you are less likely to receive adequate responses. In addition, with e-mail it is sometimes difficult to convince participants that their responses are anonymous. When deciding how the survey should be delivered, consider the format and the specific audience. The survey results are important and are worth the time and effort it takes.

The results of the needs assessment survey should provide information regarding the current expertise level of the targeted participants. It is often easy to misinterpret people's technical comfort level because many do not share their inexperience or lack of exposure to technology. If the training is planned on a level too advanced for the participants, they will become frustrated and discouraged. In contrast, if the training is planned on a level far below the participants' abilities (e.g., introducing a previously learned skill), they will believe they are wasting their time and may feel insulted or slighted. However, if the training is approached both at an appropriate level and as an opportunity for the participants to take their existing skills to a higher level, they will be more likely to attend with an open and eager attitude. The information obtained from the survey data will also indicate whether some participants should be grouped together and whether separate trainings need to occur. It may also indicate the possibility of developing mentors or support people within the faculty to assist others.

The information from the assessment tool should be compiled and shared among the planning committee members. Although it is not possible to meet all the needs of every faculty member, the commonalities should be identified. It is important not to assume the abilities of all participants. The committee members should determine how the identified needs fit into the general goal. At this time, the specific outcomes needed for the project should become evident. These specific goals may be as simple as teaching participants to become familiar with how to operate an interactive whiteboard. In some cases, it is important to spend time building foundation knowledge when it comes to technology. Do not assume knowledge or skill level. Instead, determine the baseline of knowledge and expertise. The goals may then be expanded and developed to include more in-depth training. Once teachers have been provided an opportunity to build a comfort level with the technology, they will be better able to understand how to integrate the technology into the curriculum. This is an important step because without a strong comfort level and understanding of function and purpose, reform and sustainability will not take place.

Depending on the focus and goals of the project, it might be helpful to compile a technology inventory (see Appendix B). It is sometimes amazing to see the hardware and software that can emerge out of closets, off top shelves, and from under desks. It is also nice to have a complete list of what is available as the plan develops. Although this information is often in the form of a district or state required inventory sheet, it does not always sort the hardware in a clear and usable format. Often existing materials can be put to work in more appropriate ways, so new equipment does not need to be purchased. When funding is limited, it is sometimes better to allocate dollars to providing time and teacher support so that strategies may be better integrated into the curriculum.

Now is the time to look closely at all identified and expected outcomes of the professional development and determine their feasibility and time frame. The specific goals need to be divided into short-term and long-term goals. If all the goals appear to be short-term, it is helpful to assign a skill level to each goal. For example, the short-term goal might be introducing faculty to a skill, and the long-term goal might be to develop faculty proficiency in integrating the skill into classroom instruction. As goals are established, it is important for participants to believe the project is sustainable and a valuable investment of their time. Unfortunately, many professional development plans are short-term and appear to be "here today, gone tomorrow." But if the specific goals meet the majority of the needs of the participants, are measurable, and are aligned to standards, the planning process will be built on a strong foundation. Teachers will be more likely to see an opportunity to be successful, and they will be more motivated to model what they have learned. Of course, this requires follow-up and support, which are described in subsequent chapters.

This discussion of categorizing goals may seem redundant as it was addressed in the pre-planning process discussed in the preceding chapter. However, the importance of this step cannot be overemphasized. It is sometimes difficult to see a clear connection of specific activities to the intended outcome when separating short-term and long-term goals. If the plan seems overwhelming and more involved than expected, step back and approach the project from the opposite side. Determine the one or two main measurable goals that need to be accomplished when all is said and done. Then review and fine-tune the short-term goals while eliminating those that are not necessary or could be put off and revisited at a later date. Another option is to prioritize short-term goals or include them if an interim needs assessment determines they need to be included. Some goals may need to be aligned to specific groups as opposed to targeting all participants. For example, teachers may be targeted for the first implementation, but resource teachers and assistants may be able to receive training at a different time. In other words, the short-term and long-term goals must be realistic and affordable regarding time and effort. Prioritization and elimination may be painful, but it does not have to be fatal to the plan if it is done with purpose and goals in mind.

Developing a Technology Plan

When both the short-term and the long-term goals have been established based on the focus of the project and the needs of the faculty and students, a formal technology plan should be developed. In some cases, a required district technology plan format may be provided. If not, a technology plan should still be carefully developed to include specific steps. This is important to ensure that all participants understand the goals, the process to achieve those goals, how long it will take to achieve them, and how the achievement will be evaluated.

A general Technology Plan Guide (at the end of this chapter and in Appendix B) is provided. By following these guidelines, a more specific, formal technology plan will evolve that will be aligned to and include previously identified short-term and long-term goals. It is necessary to go through the previous activity of focusing specifically on goals in order not to confuse individual activities (or actions) with more long-term goals when they are actually part of the bigger picture. In other words, it might appear that training teachers how to use interactive whiteboards or how to create and use wiki personal Web pages is a goal. However, these are instead short-term activities that address the goal of increasing student achievement in a specific area through the use of these technologies. The individual activities or implementation activities will become apparent as steps in the development process of the technology plan. Depending on the scope of the long-term goals, multiple specific technology plans may develop. In essence, the overall technology plan consists of long-term goals and short-term activities that build a foundation for the success of the long-term goals.

As the plan is developed, it is important to consider a realistic timeline for the implementation, follow up/support, and evaluation. Too often, the implementation is planned without regard to the other pieces of the puzzle. Be clear and specific in the technology plan as to which goals are long-term and which goals are short-term in order to ensure success. It is much easier to attain a goal when small steps are taken. It is also easier to feel success and to evaluate a project when it is broken down into smaller, more realistic pieces. As the steps in the process emerge, it will be easier to determine short-term plans as part of the bigger picture. For example, one short-term plan may be to acquire and install the hardware and infrastructure for the project, and another may address only the training and development of support for the project. As these short-term plans are developed, be sure to keep the long-term goal in mind so no pieces of the process are excluded.

Another example might be to teach language arts teachers to use blogs or wikis to encourage their students to write. This short-term goal would have multiple activities to include the introduction of the skill, the building of proficiency, and then the integration of the skill into existing language arts instruction. These are all part of the long-term goal of increasing student achievement in language arts. While these examples are simple, it will be easy to see that small activities will build a foundation for successfully achieving the long-term goal. The sequential process of building on skills and completing short-term goals make it easier to not only be successful but also provide sustainable professional development. It will also make assessment of success easier.

In order to help clarify this process, the two samples of pre-planning worksheets from the previous chapter have been taken through the next step in the process. Each sample has been expanded to show how the discussion from the pre-planning step evolves into the development of a more specific technology plan encompassing the activities of the short-term goals. The completion and success of these activities will support the completion of the long-term goals.

Long-Term Plan and Short-Term Plan Sample 1

This sample follows the Pre-Planning Worksheet from the previous chapter. After the pre-planning process has been completed, the long-term plan needs to be addressed. In the sample, the long-term goals were selected from the pre-planning process and used as the focus for determining the steps needed to accomplish these goals. In this case, the two goals are tied together. In some plans, there may be only one major long-term goal. However, remember that goals can easily overlap, as short-term goals can provide a foundation on which to build a more sustainable long-term goal. In the sample provided, activities in the long-term plan represent multiple short-term goals that need to be accomplished to provide this foundation. These activities may be general or detailed depending on the plan. For example, the plan for training will be part of the pre-planning and needs assessment discussion. The training activities may need to be broken down into several small sequences of activities based on the needs of participants. Another example of this is the last activity listed, which indicates "follow up and support activities." This activity will become a separate short-term plan that will include activities that may need to be refined after being carefully assessed. The short-term plan will include such activities as a needs assessment, additional training for new employees, more in-depth training for some faculty/staff, and additional support as needed. These will evolve relative to the nature of the learning community and the environment.

The short-term plan sample combines two of the activities from the long-term plan to create a plan that can be accomplished within a year. It is preferable to keep short-term plans within the academic year because of multiple issues such as available funding, student populations, and change in personnel. Note that the first two activities listed would take place simultaneously. While considering what type of interactive whiteboards will best provide activities necessary to meet the language arts curriculum requirements, it is important to consider what wiring or additional hardware (computers, etc.) will be needed. The cost and feasibility of the entire project must be considered. The least expensive solution might not have the capability needed for implementing curriculum lessons, in which case the pre-planning and original goals should be revisited. The big picture and measurable goals should always be the underlying consideration. As mentioned above, when developing the short-term plan for follow up and support, the needs assessment may reveal the level of needs are different than originally planned. More faculty turnover may have an influence on future training and support needs. Therefore, the plans must be periodically reviewed and revised based on the progress of the project.

Long-Term Plan and Short-Term Plan Sample 2

This sample relates to the second sample provided in the previous chapter and is different in that it focuses on the selection of appropriate software and training of faculty and staff to use the software in the classroom. In this case, the long-term goals are listed in order of priority. The most important goal is to improve ninth-grade student math skills. Since the school has decided that integrating math software into the curriculum will help provide a more visual and up-to-date medium for delivering math instruction, the administration must consider the use of technology as a long-term goal. This is a very credible long-term goal as it aligns with the twenty-first-century skills and supports considerable research-based instruction.

It is important for the leadership team to consider the learning community and the environment as they develop the short-term plans. This sample relates strongly on motivating the faculty as well as the students in an area that can have a considerable amount of resistance. The sustainability of using the software integrated into the curriculum and continuing to help support math instruction with technology are dependent upon the effectiveness of the professional development. In the Long-Term Technology Plan Sample 2 provided, the activities are listed very simply. It may be important to allow more time for selection of the appropriate software if time is needed to receive feedback from all faculty and staff involved. To be successful, this sample case requires as much buy-in and support from the participants as possible. It is also important to make sure the software is accessible in all areas as needed before teacher training takes place. The plan may also need to include modeling along with training, and/or implementation may need to be broken down into smaller steps than originally planned, based on the acceptance of the participants. The short-term plan will indicate each of the detailed steps needed and should be revisited frequently as the project progresses.

These two samples are provided to help clarify and enhance the discussions that must take place throughout the process of developing a plan. Not all parts of the template are completed in the samples, as areas such as resources are project specific and not necessary for clarification of the overall process. These are "living plans," if you will, as they may need to be revisited and revised as the process continues. Being flexible is an important criterion; however, it is also important to have a plan and make sure it is aligned to the overall goals. Otherwise, time and effort is spent on unnecessary activities, and some activities may have to be repeated. Strong plans will create a project that is not only cost-effective but also sustainable.

Chapter Summary—Checklist

- ☐ The focus of the project is determined.
- ☐ An administrator shares the major focus with all stakeholders.
- ☐ A planning committee is established with representatives from all areas involved.
- ☐ A leader or facilitator is identified to coordinate the planning committee.
- ☐ The committee members determine general goals.
- ☐ A needs assessment survey is developed and distributed to all stakeholders.
- ☐ Data is collected from the assessment tool and commonalities are identified.
- ☐ Specific goals are identified and determined to be short-term or long-term based on the allowed timeline.
- ☐ The planning committee develops an all-inclusive technology plan, which may include a series of specific long-term and short-term technology plans depending on the scope of the project.
- ☐ The planning committee shares the technology plan with all stakeholders with an explanation of the data collected and requests feedback.

Sample Worksheets/Templates/Guides

- Technology Plan Guide 41
- Technology Inventory 43
- Long-Term Technology Plan Template 44
- Long-Term Technology Plan Sample 1 45
- Long-Term Technology Plan Sample 2 46
- Short-Term Technology Plan Template 47
- Short-Term Technology Plan Sample 1 50
- Short-Term Technology Plan Sample 2 53

Technology Plan Guide

This guide is designed to help you gather and compile information to support the development of a short-term and a long-term technology plan. The following areas should be discussed and shared with any stakeholders. The compiled information should include:

I. **Goals/visions**
   A. Using the needs assessment survey or similar instrument, collect information focusing on the professional development needs and/or the infrastructure needs of:
      1. Faculty/staff status
         a. Beginning level
         b. Intermediate level
         c. Advanced/support level
      2. Infrastructure status—software, hardware
      3. Training needs based on status and project expectations (goals)
      4. Infrastructure needs based on project expectations (goals)
   B. Define a collaborative goal/vision for your technology plan. Develop a clear focus and be sure of the following:
      1. Be specific and clear when writing your goals.
      2. Be realistic and divide your goals into short-term and long-term in order to accomplish them in a realistic time frame.
      3. Make your goals measurable so progress and success can be determined.
      4. Consider roadblocks such as policies, funds, etc. to make sure goals are attainable.

II. **Actions**
   A. List all activities, and categorize them based on professional development, purchases, or installation. (Be specific based on your goals.)
   B. Reorganize activities sequentially in each category. Some may overlap and be ongoing. Identify these as such.
   C. Determine if actions can be divided into short-term or long-term actions. Some actions may reoccur in a long-term plan.
   D. These actions may be revisited at any time. It is better to include all activities and adjust them as the plan is redefined.

III. **Resources**
   A. Determine all resources that are available or needed. Consider human resources (support) as well as materials.
   B. When considering costs, indicate possible and realistic sources for funds.
   C. When considering human resources, indicate roles and responsibilities
   D. Review actions and make sure all actions have resources aligned to them.
   E. Consider incentives for professional development as resources needed. These do not necessarily need to be monetary in nature, but they may need approval or human resource support.

IV. **Evaluation**

    A. Define how the success of the goals will be measured and what method will be used to determine the level of success.

    B. Indicate a timeline for evaluation, and set realistic dates. Identify the purpose and what information may be determined for each evaluation.

    C. Consider a midproject evaluation to provide insight as to whether goals need to be adjusted, additional resources need to be provided, human resources need to be realigned, etc.

    D. Depending on the goal of your project, consider evaluation from students as well as from faculty and staff. This can often provide additional perspectives and resources not previously considered.

Technology Inventory

It is important during planning to have a complete inventory of all the relevant hardware, software, and other resources that are available. Many of these resources may be listed on previously completed inventories. However, the older inventories may not be complete or current. "Support" includes repair or missing parts that are needed such as cords or ink for printers. The following should be completed with the project goals and implementation plan in mind. Customize this table to meet the criteria of your plan.

I.   Hardware

Hardware	Number Available	Location	Responsible Person/Dept.	Support Needed?
1.				
2.				
3.				

II.   Software

Software	License/Access Available	Location	Responsible Person/Dept.	Support Needed?
1.				
2.				
3.				

Long-Term Technology Plan Template

Identify goals and activities that closely align to the school improvement plan or other district initiative. These goals should be long-term (more than one year). Depending on your alignment of goals, it may be better to use a spreadsheet for the responses for I, II, and III.

I.   School goal(s):

II.   Above goal(s) aligned to (school improvement plan, district initiative, grant, etc.):

III. Assessment/evaluation method/data (quantitative and measurable):

IV.   Sequential short-term technology plans/activities:

Goal	Activity Overview	Date	Location	Participants	Coordinator/ Responsible Person

Long-Term Technology Plan Sample 1

Identify goals and activities that closely align to the school improvement plan or other district initiative. These goals should be long-term (more than one year). Depending on your alignment of goals, it may be better to use a spreadsheet for the responses for I, II, and III.

I. School goal(s):
   1. Increase language arts skills for students in grades three to five
   2. Increase the use of technology integration into classroom curriculum

II. Above goal(s) aligned to (school improvement plan, district initiative, grant, etc.):
   Both goals aligned to the twenty-first century goals. Goal #1 aligned to the school improvement plan

III. Assessment/evaluation method/data (quantitative and measurable):
   Goal #1: Standardized test scores for students in grades three through five, student nine-week grades
   Goal #2: Survey of teachers, observation of teachers by administration, review of lesson plans

IV. Sequential short-term technology plans/activities (Continue this chart to include appropriate activities to address Goal #1. This is a sample of activities for Goal #2.)

Goal	Activity Overview	Date	Location	Participants	Coordinator/ Responsible Person
2	Review, select, and install appropriate interactive whiteboards (Smart Board, Promethian board, etc.)	Summer and fall	School	Leadership team, technology coordinator, principal	Leadership team facilitator
2	Train all classroom teachers how to use selected hardware and software	Spring and summer (following installation)	Computer lab and classrooms	All grade 3-5 teachers, resource, and/ or curriculum support teachers	Leadership team facilitator and technology coordinator
2	Provide modeling in classrooms and in-depth math support using technology	Fall and spring of year 2	Classrooms	All trained faculty and staff	Curriculum resource persons, leadership team facilitator
2	Follow-up and support activities	Summer and ongoing	Classrooms	All faculty, staff, and administration	Leadership team, resource and support persons

Long-Term Technology Plan Sample 2

Identify goals and activities that closely align to the school improvement plan or other district initiative. These goals should be long-term (more than one year).

I., II., and III. *(These were combined in a spreadsheet format for better visual alignment)*

I. Goals	II. Standard, objective, etc. met by goal	III. Assessment/ evaluation instrument
1. Increase math scores for at-risk ninth-grade students	School improvement plan	Standardized test scores
	District improvement plan for AYP	Final math grades
2. Increase use of technology in the classroom by math teachers	Twenty-first-century skills	Observation by administration
	School improvement plan	Survey of classroom teachers, students, and resource faculty

IV. Sequential short-term technology plans/activities (Sample addresses only activities for Goal #2 above.)

Goal	Activity Overview	Date	Location	Participants	Coordinator/ Responsible Person
2	Review, select, purchase and install appropriate math software	Summer through fall	Classrooms for all at-risk math students (including resource rooms)	All math teachers, resource teachers, and support staff working with any math students	Leadership team facilitator, technology coordinator, district technology support, vendor
2	Train teachers to use software within the classroom for instruction	Spring	Classrooms and resource rooms	All math faculty, resource, and support staff	Leadership team facilitator, vendor/trainer
2	Model integration of software into classroom instruction, and mentor faculty	Spring through the following year	Classrooms and resource rooms	All math faculty, resource, and support staff	Leadership team facilitator, all math faculty, including resource and support staff

Short-Term Technology Plan Template

This Short-Term Technology Plan should be focused and very specific. Modify the type of training and goals based on your own individual focus.

I.   Needs assessment data (from Needs Assessment Survey)
      A. Infrastructure needs
           1. Equipment (computers, printers, projectors, etc.)
           2. Software
           3. Services/support (installation, etc.)
      B. Professional development
           1. Faculty/staff needing professional development

Training (examples)	Faculty/Staff Number	Position
Beginning		
Intermediate		
Advanced		
Software		
Hardware		

II.   Goals/vision
      A. Overall long-term goal

      B. Short-term (one year or less) goal(s) (One or two of these should be selected from the Long-Term Technology Plan)

      C. Student impact expectation

      D. Faculty/staff impact expectation

III.   Action plan (List *all* activities sequentially.) (Year 1 plan)

Action/Activity	Date Beginning	Date Ending	Participants	Responsible Person(s)

IV. Resources (List *all* resources needed to accomplish the short-term goal.)

Resource Needed	Source	Funding Needed	Funding Source	Responsible Party/ Person(s)
1.				
2.				
3.				
4.				

V. Evaluation (Each goal or activity indicated in section III should be addressed in this section.)

Goals/Activities	Action Needed	Measurement Method	Documentation Needed	Date of Evaluation
1.				
2.				
3.				
4.				

Short-Term Technology Plan Sample 1

This Short-Term Technology Plan should be focused and very specific. Modify the type of training and goals based on your own individual focus.

I.   Needs assessment data (from Needs Assessment Survey)
    A. Infrastructure needs
        1. Equipment (computers, printers, projectors, etc.)
        2. Software
        3. Services/support (installation, etc.)
    B. Professional development
        1. Faculty/staff needing professional development

Training (examples)	Faculty/Staff Number	Position
Beginning		
Intermediate		
Advanced		
Software		
Hardware		

II.   Goals/vision
    A. Overall long-term goal
       • *Increase language arts skills for students in grades three to five*
       • *Increase the use of technology integration into classroom curriculum*

    B. Short-term (one year or less) goal(s) (One or two of these should be selected from the Long-Term Technology Plan)
       1. Review, select, and install appropriate interactive whiteboards (Smart board, Promethian board, etc.)
       2. Train all classroom teachers how to use selected hardware and software

    C. Student impact expectation
       Students will be motivated by the addition of technology in the classroom as observed by teachers.

    D. Faculty/staff impact expectation
       Classroom teachers, resource and support staff will be able to activate the technology in the classroom and be able to manipulate the software.

III. Action plan (List all activities sequentially.) (Year 1 plan)

Action/Activity	Date Beginning	Date Ending	Participants	Responsible Person(s)
1. Review all interactive whiteboards, and determine appropriate vendor based on capability and funds.	Summer and fall			
2. Consider hardware needs (wiring, etc.), contract with vendor, and schedule installation.	Summer and fall			
3. Determine training needs, participants, location, etc.	Fall			
4. Schedule training following installation.	Spring			
5. Schedule mentoring, support, and resource access to coincide with training.	Spring			
6. Assess short-term goals, and determine additional needs.	Late spring			

IV.   Resources (List *all* resources needed to accomplish the short-term goal.)

Resource Needed	Source	Funding Needed	Funding Source	Responsible Party/ Person(s)
1.				
2.				
3.				
4.				

V.   Evaluation (Each goal or activity indicated in section III should be addressed in this section.)

Goals/Activities	Action Needed	Measurement Method	Documentation Needed	Date of Evaluation
1.				
2.				
3.				
4.				

Short-Term Technology Plan Sample 2

This Short-Term Technology Plan should be focused and very specific. Modify the type of training and goals based on your own individual focus.

I.   Needs assessment data (from Needs Assessment Survey)
    A. Infrastructure needs
        1. Equipment (computers, printers, projectors, etc.)
        2. Software
        3. Services/support (installation, etc.)
    B. Professional development
        1. Faculty/staff needing professional development

Training (examples)	*Faculty/Staff Number*	*Position*
Beginning		
Intermediate		
Advanced		
Software		
Hardware		

II. Goals/vision
    A. Overall long-term goal
       • *Increase math scores for at-risk ninth-grade students*
       • *Increase use of technology in the classroom by math teachers*

    B. Short-term (one year or less) goal(s) (One or two of these should be selected from the Long-Term Technology Plan)
        1. *Review, select, purchase, and install appropriate math software*
        2. *Train teachers to use software within the classroom for instruction*
        3. *Model integration of software into classroom instruction, and mentor faculty*

    C. Student impact expectation
       Ninth-grade students will demonstrate increased math skills as indicated on specific math assessments.

    D. Faculty/staff impact expectation
       Ninth-grade math teachers and resource math teachers will integrate math curriculum with appropriate technology to support student achievement in math.

III.   Action plan (list *all* activities sequentially.) (Year 1 plan)

Action/Activity	Date Beginning	Date Ending	Participants	Responsible Person(s)
1. Assess critical target areas for student math skills; review appropriate software options and vendors (based on funding and hardware)	Summer and fall			
2. Select, contract with vendor, and upgrade hardware, etc., if necessary. Install software.	Summer and fall			
3. Determine training needs, participants, location for access, etc.	Fall			
4. Schedule training following installation.	Spring			
5. Schedule modeling, support, and resource access to coincide with training.	Spring			
6. Assess short-term goals, and determine additional needs.	Late spring			

IV. Resources (List *all* resources needed to accomplish the short-term goal.)

Resource Needed	Source	Funding Needed	Funding Source	Responsible Party/ Person(s)
1.				
2.				
3.				
4.				

V. Evaluation (Each goal or activity indicated in section III should be addressed in this section.)

Goals/Activities	Action Needed	Measurement Method	Documentation Needed	Date of Evaluation
1.				
2.				
3.				
4.				

5 Implementation: The Action

Implementing a plan for professional development in technology is an important step and often receives much attention. While the importance of providing quality training and professional development cannot be overestimated, the steps must be evaluated and developed within the context of the goals of the project. Too often, professional development and training are synonymous in focus and exclude all the other steps within the process. Without the other pieces of the puzzle in place, the implementation may be a waste of time, energy, and funding because the goals are not met. For example, imagine a school district technology coordinator purchased two digital cameras for each school for classroom use because additional funds became available. A one-hour training after school at the school district main office was immediately offered to any faculty or staff member who was interested in using the cameras once they arrived. Several teachers from each school attended the training. When the cameras were delivered to the schools several months later, they were placed in the media center for safekeeping and easy checkout by faculty and staff. Guess what? One year later the cameras were still sitting on the shelf; only a few of them had been checked out even once or twice. Why were they not being used? At the time of the training, the cameras were not yet available in the schools. No expectations or goals were made evident to participants attending training, so teachers did not have a personal motivation to take the time necessary to integrate this tool into classroom instruction. In addition, principals neither announced the availability of the cameras nor endorsed the cameras to indicate they were of value. With a little planning, collaboration, and time, teachers could have been using the digital cameras to make social studies, science, or math lessons more meaningful. Interestingly enough, no additional funding would have needed to be allocated in order to improve this learning opportunity. This is a simple example of training in isolation. It is not an example of effective training nor is it an example of sustainable professional development. The dollars appeared to be well spent; however, the implementation was ineffective.

The timeline for the implementation process can be as critical as the actual training activities. The appropriate hardware, software, materials, and planning must be in place prior to implementation to ensure the training will not need to be repeated. Having to repeat training can incur added expense and steal valuable time. It can also produce a negative attitude among participants who believe their time has been wasted. In addition, a rushed timeline for implementation may indicate to participants that the project has little credibility. If participants perceive the training activities as inadequate, poorly planned, and not personally beneficial, the project will have difficulty building momentum to accomplish the desired goal. In order for the implementation process to be effective, it must not be rushed and must be a relevant part of a goal addressing critical needs supporting student achievement. More importantly, awareness and clear connection to the goal must be evident during the training.

Collaboration

Collaborating with all participants involved in the project is critical. This is not to say each step in the process must become an issue voted on by the identified faculty. However, it is important to give everyone involved an opportunity to share their concerns. This may be done in the form of a survey, a comment box, e-mails, blogs, wikis, etc. Every concern and suggestion should be reviewed, and then decisions should be made by the majority of the stakeholders, as long as those decisions meet the goals and criteria of the project. Clear communication to the participants regarding the goals of the project can often help them focus their concerns and be more constructive with their feedback. Often, dissent from the faculty of a project comes primarily from a lack of understanding of the guidelines and restrictions. For example, a school improvement plan may identify the need to increase writing skills of fourth-grade students as a long-term goal. A specific technology plan may address the short-term goal of purchasing interactive whiteboards, electronic tablets, or e-books, and include training faculty on how to use the new hardware. The implementation activities may include training all fourth-grade teachers in the use of the specific hardware. Dissent and animosity may develop among the faculty if they see funds being used for technology that they feel should be spent on basic needs such a paper and pencils. This can happen with faculty who feel they have not been included in the development of the plan and do not understand how technology can better support students' writing skills. Uninformed faculty may not connect the activity with the intended goal. Collaboration prior to training will help teachers better understand how the purchase and training in the use of a specific technology can improve student writing skills. It is not always the hardware that improves student learning; it can be the mere fact that students and teachers are more motivated to be involved in learning. Yet it is sometimes difficult to separate the tools from the actions.

Decisions about implementation are sometimes made without obtaining all relevant information and outside-the-box ideas. It may be helpful to set up a location to share progress of the project and allow comments. This may be done in the form of a newsletter, a Web site, a wiki, a blog, or even a simple bulletin board. If the location is available to everyone, it will become part of everyday conversation and an integral part of the school activities.

Collaboration is a key concept. Do not confuse collaboration and the sharing of ideas with explaining and informing faculty of an upcoming activity. There is a difference between informing the faculty what will happen and asking them for feedback and suggestions. True collaboration provides opportunities for total involvement, sharing, and brainstorming with acceptance and without fear of consequences. When a project is announced but not revisited until completed, the project appears to be for the chosen few and those who are not kept informed may be insulted, and, consequently, resistant to participating in future activities. Do not underestimate the importance of faculty perception. Too often, I have watched administrators avoid sharing information with faculty because they want to shield the faculty from all the work, details, or problems. This is often detrimental. Sharing information does not necessarily mean delegating work. Collaboration and sharing build a better foundation than avoidance and secrecy—even when information is withheld with good intentions.

Scheduling

Through the use of the Needs Assessment Survey (available at the end of Chapter 3 and in Appendix B), which is developed during the planning stage, the needs should be broken down into short-term projects. These projects or activities were identified earlier and listed on the long-term technology plan. They then were broken down as specific short-term technology plans. During the implementation process, the short-term plan is molded into a working schedule that will be realistic and obtainable based on the targeted participants. This professional development process is critical, as it influences both the work schedules and the personal time of the faculty and staff. The collection of data from the survey should provide adequate information regarding the level of expertise of the participants. Be sure this survey is customized to provide the information needed for developing comprehensive and effective training sessions. This is the time to decide whether training should be done in phases and whether different levels of training should be done multiple times. If the professional development does not meet the needs of the participants, the project will be less successful.

Divide the training sessions into different levels if possible. The results of the needs assessment may indicate a vast range of ability levels regarding technical skills. In this case, it may be necessary to provide an introductory workshop for teachers with little or no background to increase their comfort level. Depending on the project, an overview might be done for all participants in the form of a mini-training with more in-depth training to follow. Training sessions might also need to be divided in other ways. For example, the goal may require multiple teachers from different content areas to be involved in training activities. In this case, teachers with a similar focus should be grouped together so they can share and mentor each other. This will provide for more meaningful professional development in a shorter period of time. A large, diverse group of teachers attempting to work together can sometimes be less effective than groups with common interests. For example, in my experience, a fifth-grade science teacher does not have the same concerns as a kindergarten teacher. Because of this, small, focused trainings are often more effective and better received. Small trainings also allow for and encourage collaboration.

Depending on the number of participants, it may be easier to provide an overview and basic training for everyone and then provide additional small workshops customized to certain participants' needs. When deciding which categories of training sessions are needed, look at the number of participants falling into each category. Small group trainings are often easier to schedule, less costly, and more effective. A one-hour focused training can sometimes be more effective than a three- or four-hour drawn-out training. A training schedule overview and two sample training schedules (see Appendix B) are provided to help give you ideas. Overall, quality is more important than quantity. Many have incorrectly believed that a few large trainings will cover everyone and "get it done." However, this approach will lead participants to ask for more support and retraining to develop their comfort levels and fill in the gaps. Participants should not leave a training feeling it was a waste of time because of level, content, or inconvenient scheduling. Large trainings also often leave participants feeling that they have to take the information obtained from the workshop and learn the software or hardware on their own. While practice is important, if the participants are not comfortable enough after the training, they will not attempt to practice on their own. Small groups working together tend to solve this problem.

Sharing the training schedule with participants prior to finalization will help improve participants' awareness and help them feel part of the process. They will attend each training session with a more positive outlook and be ready to learn. To my dismay and frustration, I have sometimes begun workshops (after being hired by the principal) only to discover in the first few minutes that many of the attending teachers were not informed of the training until they arrived at school that morning and found substitutes in their classrooms. With little or no information about the goal, expectations, or content of the training, the teachers were not motivated to participate in it. Teachers need a positive learning environment as much as students do.

Training Process

It is important to give some thought to the actual training process. Some administrators decide to hire outside consultants to provide the training. Although this is sometimes necessary to ensure participants receive quality training, it is also important that administrators and/or members of the planning team be involved with the process of teacher training. As previously mentioned, training sessions should be divided into categories based on a needs assessment. Each session should then be planned in order to provide teachers with sufficient skills and a comfort level to meet the expectations of the goals. Carefully consider the following key elements of the training process.

Hands-On Training

It is critical to have adequate equipment and materials for all participants to work independently. Ideally, this equipment is the same teachers will be expected to use in the classroom. Mirroring the expected environment as much as possible is important for success because many adults are not adaptable when it comes to technology. Any hardware or software training where teachers are expected to be able to integrate the skills into their teaching and develop a comfort level of use will not be successful if teachers are not provided the opportunity to explore independently. Sometimes teachers offer to work with other teachers so they do not to have to work on a computer and display their lack of comfort with technology. These are the very people who need to have their own equipment and materials.

Time

It is important to schedule enough time for formal training so that teachers can receive the necessary information and apply their knowledge with input and support from the instructor. Additional time should be provided following training with support for teachers to develop their comfort level (e.g., schedule times when a computer lab is available or specific times when resource or mentor teachers may be available to answer questions). Be careful not to make the training too long so teachers feel time was not wasted. The two sample training schedules (see Appendix B) may be a good place to start. As mentioned previously, they both demonstrate how multiple one- to two-hour small sessions can be scheduled to more effectively use people's time. With these schedules, faculty can attend small, focused trainings rather than one large, full-day training. The additional help sessions assist teachers who need to build their comfort level. Full-day trainings are often disliked because of such issues as:

- ◆ Teachers are away from their students all day.
- ◆ Time is lost for lunch, breaks, and other school interruptions.
- ◆ Many substitutes (if even available) in a school can be very disruptive to the school.
- ◆ The amount of content covered in a full day can be overwhelming to participants.

In multiple short trainings, more can often be accomplished with fewer people. In addition, multiple trainings allow participants to absorb and practice what they have learned between trainings.

Two sample training schedule forms are provided at the end of this chapter and in the appendix. Sample Training Schedule A is focused on providing one- to two-hour blocks for training during the instructional day without using substitutes. The same template is designed to collect data and target training times that take into account common planning periods to allow teachers with a common focus to work together. The sample reveals that some teachers are willing to train before and/or during their planning time (second and fourth grade) and some are willing to train after school and/or during their planning time (third and fifth grade). This information will make it easier to develop an acceptable training schedule. Sample Training Schedule B takes into account an efficient way to make use of a few substitutes during the instructional day and still provide small, one- or two-hour focused trainings. The schedule uses substitutes to their maximum so more teachers can take advantage of the short, focused training periods. The substitutes move from classroom to classroom, allowing teachers to attend training. By combining planning periods, it may be possible to have a flexible lunch schedule as well as a smoother transition. This type of schedule can be time intensive in the planning stage, but it can be an efficient way to use time and dollars.

As adult learners, teachers prefer to be given all the required information, have the goals and expectations clearly explained and reinforced, and then have the ability to develop their own skills on a personal level. Give some thought to how much time is needed to cover the information and allow for collaboration without dragging out the process.

Individual Differences

The implementation process needs to address the varying skill levels of the participants. Although the software training or required skill may be new to all teachers, the overall level of experience with technology can vary considerably. Thus, it may be helpful to pair technology-experienced teachers with those who have less experience. Being aware of these differences will help improve the comfort level of the less experienced, potentially insecure participants. When planning training sessions that are curriculum specific, it is important to consider the individual focus of the participants. For example, if the training is focused on improving student math skills, participants who are English teachers may not feel the training is necessary for them. If the intention is for a cross-curricular approach, this direction should be made clear before the implementation activities to ensure acceptance from faculty. A small group training for English teachers may be more effective and provide them an opportunity to discuss specific needs and strategies appropriate for their students. A combined meeting of the two groups could be scheduled later. Also, be considerate of teachers' individual focus, such as addressing students with special needs or diverse student populations, or providing differentiated instruction in the classroom.

Access

The availability of specific hardware and software may have a critical impact on the success of an implementation. If teachers are provided training, but the software is not available in their classroom or even their school, the implementation may need to be repeated. For example, if the plan is to install interactive whiteboards in all math classrooms, but only one has been installed thus far, the training should not be scheduled until all have been installed. If teachers leave the training and are not able to immediately use the whiteboards to practice, they'll be asking for additional training or more instruction when the whiteboards are installed in their classrooms. Do not rush the implementation schedule for the sake of the overall project. In some cases, and if at all possible, it would be beneficial for teachers to have access to the software and/or materials from home. This may be easy, depending on the software and vendor resources. Having home access allows teachers the opportunity to work at their own pace.

Location

Finding an adequate location for training is often a problem. Many districts prefer to have teachers leave their own schools and attend training in a central location. Although this can make training easier and eliminate many school-based interruptions, most teachers prefer not to travel. Furthermore, scheduling training in the home school allows teachers to be trained on familiar equipment in a comfortable location. Teachers are more likely to continue to practice their new skills or explore the software if they are comfortable and feel they can replicate the training environment. While providing training at the home school site may be ideal, this is not to say the training cannot be successful if it is held at a central location. Each situation must be evaluated based on time, distance, opportunity, and the goals of the plan.

Modeling

Demonstrating the expected use and implementation process is critical for participants in any training. The old adages "a picture is worth a thousand words" and "seeing is believing" hold true in this case. When teachers observe someone modeling the expected behavior, they develop a much clearer understanding of the capability of the hardware or software. This is most beneficial when the modeling can be done before, during, and following the training. For example, teachers may be receiving professional development on the use of the interactive whiteboard and be expected to integrate their new skills into classroom instruction. These teachers need to observe other teachers modeling the expected behavior with a classroom full of students. Demonstrations may be provided during the training, but it is best to also schedule visits to classrooms where teachers model the expected behavior with their students. No amount of formal training can take the place of this activity. When I have modeled the use of specific software while teaching a lesson to students in a classroom, observing teachers have commented, "Now I understand what you mean. I think I can do that." Modeling is a critical element to the implementation process and cannot be over emphasized.

Support/Resources

Once the implementation plan is formalized, thought must be given to developing the materials and resources needed to support the professional development. Consider general documents to assist users with hardware and software. Because most learners are visual, it is important to have such materials to reinforce any learning expectations. If funding or printing is an obstacle, these materials may be posted online, e-mailed to participants, or posted on a common bulletin board, wiki, or social networking Web page.

If materials are provided by a vendor, be sure to discuss the availability of these materials online. If faculty and staff are expected to use specific equipment, it may be necessary to post easy, step-by-step instructions. Being shown how to use something during training does not mean teachers or staff will be able to use it themselves after the training. All professional development should be accompanied by printed materials or electronic access to materials both during and following the training sessions. Be sure to include any samples or resources needed for clear understanding of the learning expectation.

Evaluation

When faculty or staff members are expected to spend their time and effort being involved in professional development, it is important that administrators or the providers of the implementation request feedback. This not only allows the participants to feel they are an important part of the process but also provides a valuable evaluation of the program. However, this is only a piece of the evaluation process. Administrators often determine the success of an initiative in one of three ways: a culminating activity, feedback from participants about whether they liked the training, or feedback on whether the skills or hardware are still being used after a long period of time. None of these are valid or inclusive enough to be the sole standard for evaluation.

The long-term plan and short-term plans must be revisited throughout the process. In most cases, it is primarily short-term plans that need to be adjusted. Sometimes an additional short-term plan needs to be added to the original long-term plan. The collection of information from participants and those involved in the plan will allow those who are implementing the process to improve the plan during the early stages. Information can be obtained in the form of observations, interviews, and/or surveys. In order to improve future trainings, each formally scheduled training session should conclude with a survey or questionnaire to determine not only what the participants learned but also what feedback they have to share. These varied sources all provide information about the success of the implementation. Consider obtaining feedback from students as well as teachers. Encourage teachers to self-assess and reflect on their individual progress as well as on how they've attained the goals of the technology plan. This will help coordinators as they support the process and provide needed resources and need to review and revise the plan.

Customary data collection aligned with the specific goals determined during the planning stages will be the primary culminating evaluation instrument for analysis. However, it is important to consider all the pieces of the process in order to clearly evaluate the strengths and weaknesses of the plan. Evaluation should be ongoing so the process can be revised and refined for success. It should not be all about the bottom line. If student learning has increased, great! Let's keep up the good work and continue to reform and improve the process.

Chapter Summary—Checklist

☐ Collaborate with all individuals involved in the technology plan.

☐ Provide clear communication to all regarding the plan for the implementation process and the reasons for these decisions.

☐ Schedule training based on the needs assessment survey and necessary criteria from the needs assessment survey.

☐ Plan the training process with the trainer in order to address the goals and expectations of the project.

☐ Take into account critical training areas such as hands-on training, time, individual differences, access, location, and modeling.

☐ Develop and provide adequate support materials and resources for participants in the training.

☐ Evaluate each training session as part of the short- and long-term evaluation process.

☐ Encourage ongoing evaluation and self-assessment of the process.

☐ Collect and analyze data as needed.

Sample Worksheets/Templates/Guides

♦ Training Schedule Overview 67
♦ Training Schedule A Sample. 68
♦ Training Schedule B Sample 69

Training Schedule Overview

Complete the following table by listing all trainings or professional development activities. Larger school districts may add additional similar tables for groups of trainings addressing specific district technology plans.

Targeted Goal _____

Expected Outcome _____

Measureable Assessment _____

Time Line: Begin _____   Complete _____

Date	Time	Location	Content	Expected Participants	Coordinator/ Trainer/ Responsible Person

Training Schedule A Sample

Training times of one- or two-hour blocks for focused training and/or support may be scheduled throughout the day. Use this format to develop a training schedule. These training times may be:

- ☒ before school
- ☒ after school
- ☒ planning times (specific grade levels or subject areas with common planning)
- ☐ lunch period (participants bring their own lunch)
- ☐ teacher planning or work days
- ☐ other

In order to identify available options for training, complete the following table by blocking available training times for specific groups. Customize the columns based on times teachers are willing to train (early or late) or on class period times. The grade or subject areas in the first column should be customized based on the target audience to be trained. The results of this table will indicate whether it's possible to have training/collaborative groups meet together based on grade levels or subject areas.

Grade/Group	7:00	8:00	9:00	10:00	11:00	12:00	1:00	2:00	3:00	4:00
Kindergarten							✘			
First								✘		
Second	✘				✘					
Third			✘						✘	
Fourth	✘		✘							
Fifth		✘							✘	

Training Schedule B Sample

This schedule provides a very cost-effective way to use substitute dollars for professional development. In this simple sample of a school training, four substitutes enable twelve teachers to participate in two-hour training blocks. The times may be adjusted by five to ten minutes on each side to account for movement between groups.

Begin with a blank schedule and customize columns by indicating the appropriate school times, blocks, or periods. The first column should be customized with individual teacher names. Include planning periods on the schedule to help stretch substitute time. It may be possible to cover another teacher's classroom when planning periods are taken into account. Classroom teachers and substitute teachers should eat lunch with their classes if possible; however, a lunch block is included for the coordinator/trainer. It may be necessary to build in a thirty-minute block before or after a training block to allow for lunch.

This simple schedule can be used as a framework. An after-school training for everyone can be included for follow-up, or an additional two-hour block can be added to train another group of teachers.

Teacher	8:00	9:00	10:00	11:00	12:00	1:00	2:00	3:00	4:00
A	Sub. 1	Sub. 1							
B			Sub. 1	Sub. 1					
C						Sub. 1	Sub. 1		
D	Sub. 2	Sub. 2							
E			Sub. 2	Sub. 2					
F						Sub. 2	Sub. 2		
G	Sub. 3	Sub. 3							
H			Sub. 3	Sub. 3					
I						Sub. 3	Sub. 3		
J	Sub. 4	Sub. 4							
K			Sub. 4	Sub. 4					
L						Sub. 4	Sub. 4		
Coordinator					Lunch				

6 Follow-Up and Support: Now What?

Once the implementation process of professional development has been completed, or at least the training has been completed, many coordinators will deem the project done. More often than not, reports are created, presentations made, and administrators announce the project complete and successful. Everything has been checked off the list! However, this does not mean the professional development should be determined complete or even effective. In order for professional development to influence instruction and have an impact on school reform, teachers must be both using their new skills and building on these skills. If the goals and objectives were aligned and planned well with the overall project, student achievement should become evident. In other words, there should be a measurable improvement. If there is no evidence of the implementation activities being modeled or the new skills being practiced in the classroom, it is time to revisit the technology plan. Review the original goals along with the evidence of their success. Review the short-term goals and activities to determine which were successful and which were not and why. Refer back to Figure 2.1, the Model for Effective Professional Development (page 11) and the checklists at the end of earlier chapters.

In order to provide effective professional development, the plan *must* include the key elements of follow-up and support for the participants. Without these in place, the haunting omen of "this too shall pass" and "just wait, it will go away" will come to fruition. Read the rest of this chapter and then immediately go back to add these elements into your plan. Revisit the original goals and expected outcomes. Review the evaluations and determine the strengths and weaknesses of the short- and long-term plans. Weaknesses may need to be addressed in the form of additional specific technology plans. However, they may also be improved with strong follow-up and support. Even the strengths need to be reinforced with follow-up and support.

There are a multitude of reasons that professional development often ends with the implementation process. It is easy to read the evaluations and find that the majority of participants were generally satisfied with the training and appear to be motivated by the process. However, it is important not to assume that this motivation will continue without active support and available resources.

Shortly after the implementation process, it is important to reinforce the professional development of the faculty and to provide them with an opportunity to take their skills to a higher level. This can be done in a number of ways through collaboration, sharing, and recognition of expected behaviors. With adequate support and encouragement, the faculty can begin to take charge of their own learning and create a more effective learning environment for students. Such encouragement can take the form of supporting individual faculty self-learning as opposed to supporting formal training. Providing this support can be as simple as extending already established small-group workshops for faculty. These may be expanded into discussion and sharing groups, where faculty and staff have an opportunity to share their best instructional practices in the classroom with other faculty. Collaboration is a powerful motivator even in the simplest form.

All people need to feel their efforts and feelings are validated. Activities that allow teachers to collaborate and share their successes will help teachers become more involved and encourage those who have not embraced the project. Providing additional training for teachers who are uncomfortable or allowing teachers who may have missed the training to attend a small-group training session will help validate the importance of the plan. The continued use of a needs assessment survey will help identify these additional needs and concerns. Actions can sometimes speak louder than words.

As you revisit and review the entire project, make sure this final phase is solid. It may need to be reevaluated based on the outcomes of the implementation. For example, the evaluation process may determine that more specific training is needed. As the follow-up and support plan is developed, consider the key elements below. Some may be incorporated together or even attached to another grant or project for additional support or funding, if needed. Not all support and follow-up activities require funding. At any rate, consider how each one may be addressed in your specific situation.

Support/Resource Person

It is invaluable to have a designated person responsible for answering questions, providing updates, and supporting faculty and staff on all aspects of the project. This person should be knowledgeable, or at least have access to needed information, and be available to provide support. Although, this person should ideally provide face-to-face support, this may seem like a pie-in-the-sky option. If one person must provide support from a district office or support multiple sites, it is better than having no support person at all. Sometimes this person can be another faculty/staff member who is interested and can provide part-time support. Funding is usually the issue in this case. Sometimes, having a trade-off of duties or sharing responsibilities encourages faculty members to take on this responsibility. One school I worked with asked for one teacher at each grade level to be a designated support person for their team. These support people received additional training, resources, and release time to assist their peers. In this case, the support team was a very successful resource, and teachers felt comfortable going to their team support person for assistance. The key concept is that one or more people need to be designated as "go to" people for questions and answers. While Web sites and toll-free phone numbers are wonderful resources, the majority of faculty members will not take the time to go to these for answers to what they consider "stupid" questions. More often than not, they feel comfortable asking a quick question of a peer or available resource person at their school. This same person can help keep the momentum of the project moving in a positive direction through modeling and collaboration.

Incentives

School districts and state boards of education often have mandates in place requiring teachers to participate in technology trainings, attend a minimum number of professional development hours, obtain a specific skill level to pass state exams, or demonstrate levels of expertise. These mandates might appear to be an incentive for teachers to attend professional development. In reality, however, they rarely motivate faculty to improve or increase personal skills. Research has shown that these mandates are not strong motivators in helping sustain skills. Creative incentives (e.g., recognition, conference opportunities, and the reward of extra technology for classroom use) are usually much more effective. I have been in many workshops where teachers admitted they were there because they needed the credit or were interested in the dollars they would receive (hard to believe given that it is usually very little). Such participants often lack motivation and can make the atmosphere challenging for those around them as well as for the instructor. Those who are more involved in the training and ask more questions are usually there by choice or are there for their own personal intrinsic gain.

One of the best examples of an incentive I have been involved with was the reward of a classroom projection system (projector, computer, mobile-cart system). In order to receive the system, the teacher was asked to sign a contract agreeing to attend training on specific instructional software. The teacher was also required to provide training for several other teachers in the school, invite teachers to observe him or her using the software in the classroom multiple times, and develop and document several integrated lesson plans using the system. Teachers were eager to sign up and acted as models for their peers in their schools. Because of this project, other teachers observed excellent examples of technology being integrated into the curriculum and were motivated to become involved. Schools with two or more willing participants had a faculty that had demonstrated a change in attitude toward using computers in the classroom. Teachers were proud of their new skills, motivated to develop new strategies and lessons for instruction, and thrilled with their new technology-equipped classrooms. More importantly, students were more focused and interested with the change in instructional delivery. Overall, it was a win-win incentive.

Sometimes incentives can be built into the plan, such as in Sample 2 in Chapter 4. The long-term plan was to have all math teachers integrating math software into the classroom instruction. This plan involved the installation of the software in the classroom and training for all relevant faculty members. This particular school also needed computers and projectors installed in their classrooms. Because funding was available in increments over a period of time, the district decided to provide hardware and software for half the teachers the first year and the other half the second. Therefore, teachers were asked to "apply" to receive the opportunity to be involved in the project the first year. This not only encouraged motivated teachers to participate and be the first to receive the resources but also provided model teachers for those who were participating in the second year. Sometimes what seems like a challenge can become a positive aspect of a plan.

Ongoing Support

A plan for ongoing support of the project should have been included in the initial planning stage. If it wasn't, it is not too late to revisit the long-term plan and address this issue. Ongoing support encompasses both the support provided after trainings and support when the short-term activities have been completed. Sometimes in the early stages of a project, ongoing support at the end of the project may not seem critical. It might help to look at ongoing support as insurance. It provides momentum for the goals and sustains the growth process. Planning for adequate support will make a positive difference in the value received for the time and money spent.

After the completion of what appears to be well-planned training activities, administrators will understandably anticipate the expected implementation of the new skill to continue within the classroom. For example, if teachers have attended trainings on how to use an interactive whiteboard, administrators should expect to see teachers using whiteboards in classrooms. Administrators become frustrated when they discover months later or at the beginning of the following school year that teachers are using the whiteboards as projection boards and not using their interactive capabilities. Sometimes administrators assume there was a problem with the training. This is not necessarily the case. More times than not, the implementation ended with the training, and administrators expected the goal to "just happen." As a simple follow-up, administrators could visit classrooms periodically to observe the expected instructional strategies. The presence of a support teacher modeling the behavior in classrooms can have a strong influence on the project. Also, principals sharing best practices and verbally rewarding teachers they have observed using the hardware can be a motivating factor. Reinforcing teachers for taking the initiative will encourage participation by others.

Without continued support, encouragement, and reinforcement, this lack of implementation is a common scenario. Either teachers have "forgotten" what they learned, did not develop a strong enough comfort with the technology to be self-motivated, or have questions or concerns with no one to respond to them. In some cases, teachers have transitioned to other schools or levels while new teachers have taken their place and do not have the initial knowledge. Without an effective, ongoing support plan, this can become a costly cycle. Consider how each of these trends will be addressed when developing your plan, and be sure it is still appropriate as the steps evolve.

While identifying a dedicated support/resource person in each school may be the best long-term support, it does require allocations of personnel funds, space, etc. It may also be possible to have team leaders or other key faculty play a mentoring role to maintain the support and assist changes in the faculty or staff. For example, a school may provide additional training for one person from each grade level or team within a school that expects all teachers to use interactive whiteboards. It is not always best to assign this duty to the chairperson or lead person on the team. The best person may not always be the faculty member with the most technology motivation or the one who appears to have additional or flexible time. Taking extra effort to identify the most motivated person or persons will make a difference in their success. These lead faculty members may be rewarded with the first installation of hardware or software, extra training, and additional time (if funding is available) to build their skills. In turn these leaders will be expected to support and encourage a small group of their peers. This is one positive way to provide ongoing support and modeling within a school for little money. Do not forget to provide adequate resources to support the leaders so they can accomplish the expectations established.

Materials and Resources

Resources such as user manuals, support materials, resource contact information, curriculum materials, and manipulatives should be easily accessible to all participants. Faculty and staff often believe that these materials disappear, when, in fact, they are located in the media center or on a specific teacher's bookcase. When there is turnover in faculty or staff, these items may unintentionally go with them. With the digital age, it is helpful to have as many of these materials as possible available online in one easily accessible spot. Be sure to include any lesson plans or instructional strategies developed by faculty. These are often not compiled and disseminated when they can be the most valuable of all resources. With the electronic age, it is easy to make materials and information available on Web sites, wikis, etc. While this is fine for some of the materials, many must still exist in hard copy. Therefore, location and accessibility can still be an issue, and this information should be communicated to anyone who might benefit from the materials and resources. The location of these materials should be posted where it will be a constant reminder for those who might need them (e.g., bulletin boards, newsletters, Web sites).

Periodic Review

It is important to continue to review the progress and status of the project on a regular basis. Although this should be done at a minimum of once a year, every semester or every month might be more beneficial depending on the specific goals and timeline of the activities. The assessments at the end of each professional development activity or steps in the technology plan are not the only evaluation pieces. These assessments are beneficial documents, which should be collected for analysis along with additional data. This periodic review should encompass multiple aspects of the plan to date. It should at the very least address the specific goals of the project, both short-term and long-term, and it should include multiple forms of data collection. One excellent example of obtaining data is in the form of a simple survey or follow-up needs assessment (see the end of this chapter and Appendix B). This survey, as with others mentioned, may be delivered via e-mail or as a handout during a faculty meeting. A periodic review of how the faculty and/or staff feel about their skills and needs are necessary to determine if additional support or training is needed or if the identified goals are going to be met. This review will indicate whether parts of the plan need to be revisited and revised. In the long run, this step will provide valuable information and help ensure effective professional development. A bonus of this activity and review is that it will reinforce to the faculty that this plan is important is supported by administration. Additional normal data collection from classroom assessments, observations, and student standardized data is helpful in determining the success and additional needs of the technology plan.

The sample Follow-Up Needs Assessment Survery (page 79) should be used as a basis for developing a goal-specific survey. Review the original short- and/or long-term goals of the project. Be sure to address each of the areas where feedback will be needed. This survey should be customized to collect the necessary data to help the leadership team improve, support, and help sustain the process.

Self-Assessment and Reflection

Unfortunately, self-assessment is seldom included in professional development plans. Yet it can prove very helpful in determining success or identifying changes needed. Asking participants to reflect on their experiences after the training encourages them to think about their own needs and reactions. It not only keeps the plan's goals foremost in their minds but also lets them know their opinions and experiences are valued. Completing this activity on a regular basis will help provide more honest feedback on surveys. Depending on the people and personalities involved, self-assessment and reflection can be done individually and not shared. The process alone can be beneficial. However, a good option would be to create a blog, wiki, or social networking Web site where participants could be involved in sharing and discussing successes and concerns. Some teachers prefer to participate in open discussions following grade level/team meetings or faculty meetings. A combination of options might be best, depending on the interests and comfort level of the individual school faculty and staff.

Shared Success

The opportunity for faculty to share their successes and positive experiences with their colleagues is invaluable. This can become both an incentive and a resource for others. Opportunities for sharing may be in the form of modeling the skill for others by inviting them to classrooms, sharing successful teaching strategies at faculty meetings, presenting at conferences, submitting stories to a school/district newsletter, or posting a video or a helpful hint on a school Web site, blog, or wiki. Sometimes faculty must be encouraged, as sharing does not always come naturally to them. It might be helpful to have a school "crier," so to speak, to encourage collaboration and sharing of success. The opportunities can be endless, so think creatively. This is a valuable activity, does not require funding, and takes minimal time.

This final step of follow-up and support is often the piece that is neglected or underestimated. After intensive planning and implementation, many administrators feel the professional development is complete and the skills learned should be automatically integrated into everyday classroom activity. However, this rarely is the case without additional support. Taking the time to include the key elements discussed in this chapter may mean the difference between a professional development being simply checked off the list and an effective and sustainable professional development plan. Be creative as to how you address these areas. They do not always require funding, but if they do, funding can sometimes be found through grants or willing vendors. Ideally, taking the time to plan, assess, and revisit the plan will provide more value for the money spent.

Chapter Summary—Checklist

☐ Identify a support/resource person
☐ Determine available incentives
☐ Identify and plan for long-term support
☐ Determine availability of materials/resources and where they will be located.
☐ Build into the plan a schedule for periodic review of the goals and activities.
☐ Provide opportunities for faculty to engage in self-assessment and reflection, and encourage them to participate.
☐ Provide opportunities for faculty to share successes and collaborate.

Sample Worksheets/Templates/Guides

♦   Follow-Up Needs Assessment Survey 79

Follow-Up Needs Assessment Survey

In order to determine the progress and success of the professional development and technology plans, it is important for all participants to respond to questions regarding their perception of their learning environment and future needs. These results will be helpful in the revision of the plan and in meeting future needs so the faculty can achieve their goal(s).

I have attended the following number of scheduled technology workshops this school year:

_____ 0 workshops

_____ 1 workshop

_____ 2–3 workshops

_____ 4 or more workshops (please indicate how many: _____)

Please respond to the following questions using the following scale:

1 = very uncomfortable, 2 = somewhat uncomfortable,
3 = somewhat comfortable, 4 = very comfortable

1. My comfort level using the new hardware (ex: interactive whiteboard) is: ① ② ③ ④
2. My comfort level using the new software (ex: PowerPoint) is: ① ② ③ ④
3. My comfort level integrating the new technology into my lesson plans is: ① ② ③ ④

Please respond to the following questions using the scale:

1 = never, 2 = seldom, 3 = sometimes, 4 = frequently, 5 = always

4. I believe the principal is involved and committed to providing opportunities and support for this project. ① ② ③ ④ ⑤
5. Fellow teachers, trainers, and/or support consultants are available for help when I need it. ① ② ③ ④ ⑤
6. Opportunities are provided to observe other teachers modeling the new expected skill in the classroom. ① ② ③ ④ ⑤
7. Materials and resources are available when I need them. ① ② ③ ④ ⑤
8. The goals and expectation of the project are clear. ① ② ③ ④ ⑤

Please respond to the following questions:

9. The most valuable aspects/activities of this project for me have been:

    _____

    _____

10. In order to further develop my skills, I still need:

    _____

    _____

7 Conclusion: Growing the Process

Allow me to restate my belief that this is a very exciting time to be part of education and the movement to reform our schools into a new and motivating place to learn. Every school in America, whether it is public, private, charter, magnet, large, or small is being faced with taking a closer look at how it does business. Prominent topics in recent educational journals, newsletters, professional publications, and newspapers relate to school reform and questions such as, "Are our schools educating our children to meet the needs of the twenty-first century?" and "Are our teachers prepared to teach?" The public demands more accountability in the form of evidence of better teachers and increased student achievement. While these are attention-getting buzzwords for titles and head- lines, the fact is that school administrators are feeling the pressure to produce evidence of change. The published research, standards, and guidelines (a small amount of which were referenced in Chapter 2) are forcing federal and state education boards and local school boards and parents to question what is happening in our schools. This is not some- thing that will go away with time, nor do we want it to.

The most recent data-driven argument for change in schools is that students in the United States are falling behind children in other developed nations. While this is a fact, it is also comparing oranges to apples. The more important question is, "Are our educational processes preparing our children to reach their potential?" Most schools are doing the best they can under the financial, regulatory, and control burdens they bear. Could they do better with a fresh creative look? Absolutely! As a professor in a college of education, I ask my preservice teachers to think outside the box and come up with what they think would be a perfect school. Without hidden agendas and ideas tainted with frustration of experience, it is amazing the creative programs, scheduling, and activities they share. While they do not always understand the depth required to create change, they offer many creative ideas for school reform. Interestingly enough, not all preservice teachers are technology wizards. However, they do embrace the concept that technology is a part of the twenty-first century and that students today sometimes learn more easily using these mediums. Technology is a powerful tool, which can motivate and encourage students to approach learning in new and often clearer ways.

This book is not intended to convince readers that schools must reform or that technology should be an integral piece of school change. There are a multitude of research articles and experiences to support reform. Hopefully, this book will assist schools and school districts in making the process of professional development in technology a more palatable and easier road to follow when the majority of administrators and faculty are headed in the same direction. If the stage is set, so to speak, and the environment is positive, those who are resistant will be more likely to follow along and, hopefully, be caught up in the motivation of others. The building of a community of learners and the collaboration that follows will create a much more conducive environment for reform. This is the foundation that needs to be established to make the entire process smoother. Change is more likely to take place when people are primarily moving in the same direction and believe in the cause. This is the positive learning environment necessary for the momentum of sustainable and effective professional development.

In looking at the big picture as a completed puzzle, review Figure 2.1, the Model for Effective Professional Development in Technology (page 11) for a visual interpretation. To summarize, there are three major processes: planning, implementation, and follow-up/support. Each of these processes contains multiple elements that must be considered. The degree to which each must be addressed depends on the specifics of the goals and overall focus of the plan. Do not overlook the inclusion factors at the top and bottom of the model. Administrators and faculty must have some involvement with all other stakeholders throughout the process. Again, the in-depth degree of involvement will depend upon each individual plan. Ongoing support, the use of available resources, and revision of the plan should take place throughout the entire process. These will all help establish a strong foundation for a positive learning environment. This model is provided as a guideline and as a check and balance to assist school administrators and technology coordinators as they develop their own goals and supporting activities. It is meant to be adapted to any professional development technology-based goals. My suggestion is to have these elements handy throughout the development and implementation of the entire process.

Overall, professional development must include a complete set of processes in order to provide effective and sustainable change. Although the big picture may be evident with some of the pieces in place, it will be undeniably clearer with all of the pieces in place. True school reform is not easy even if all the steps are followed.

My hope is that readers will be able to apply these processes to their own unique circumstances. However, the reality is that many district coordinators and technology directors, when faced with districtwide professional development, are not given the flexibility or authority to facilitate this process. The question sometimes is, "There is no way I have time to do all the processes in this book. Can I still be successful?" It is important to remember that the processes and elements mentioned in the book are not intended to be done by one person. One reason for an unsuccessful implementation is the expectation that one person has to do it all. That is why it is so important to build a community of learners and identify a planning committee or leadership team to collaborate and assist in putting all of the puzzle pieces in place. The coordinator should be the facilitator and motivator.

As a leader, I have often been told it is important to delegate in order to be successful. It is impossible for a single person to do everything alone, and you should not try. Chapters 3 and 4 discuss the importance of building a learning community and encouraging faculty to collaborate. Research shows that when people are completely involved in a process, they will develop buy-in and be more motivated and willing to take part in the activities. Leaders will evolve in the collaboration process. Delegation implies people are being assigned duties as opposed to being willing to accept them. If you can motivate, you will not have to delegate.

Growing the process is the responsibility of everyone involved. Hopefully, this message can be shared with all the stakeholders. Remember the original goal of any professional development is to provide an increase in student achievement. When the frustration of politics, funding concerns, personnel issues, and all the unique challenges of education appear overwhelming, try to remember that, as educators, we are all in this together working toward the same ultimate goal. We all want to improve the learning opportunities for our children. Therefore, we are all moving in the right direction. The question becomes, "How can we get there faster and more efficiently, and continue to grow the process?" Effective professional development in technology will be a big step forward toward reaching those goals.

I encourage you to take a deep breath, try not to be overwhelmed, and forge ahead with a positive attitude. It really *is* an exciting time in the history of education. As you reread these chapters, you may still have some questions. If you have more concerns or problems that have not been addressed in these pages, please feel free to contact me. Supporting schools as they reform and prepare students and teachers for a future in the twenty-first century is my passion.

Appendix A:
References and Resources

References

Andree, A., Darling-Hammond, L., Orphanos, S., Richardson, N., & Wei, R. C., (2009). *Professional learning in the learning profession: A status report on teacher development in the United States and abroad.* Dallas, TX. National Staff Development Council.

Darling-Hammond, L., Jaquith, A., Mindich, D., & Wei, R.C. (2010). *Teacher professional learning in the United States: Case studies of state policies and strategies.* Oxford, OH: Learning Forward.

Galbraith, M., Sisco, B., & Guglielmino, L. (1997). *Administering successful programs for adults.* Malabar, FL: Krieger Publishing Company.

Gray, L., Thomas, N., & Lewis, L. (2010). *Teachers' use of educational technology in U.S. public schools: 2009* (NCES 2010-040). Washington, DC: National Center for Education Statistics, Institute of Education Sciences, U.S. Department of Education.

ISTE. (2008). *National Educational Technology Standards for Teachers.* Available from http://www.iste.org/standards/nets-for-teachers/nets-for-teachers-2008.aspx.

Joyce, B., & Showers, B. (2002). *Student achievement through staff development* (3rd ed.). Alexandria, VA: Association for Supervision and Curriculum Development.

Knowles, M., & Associates. (1984). *Andragogy in action: Applying modern principles of adult learning.* San Francisco, CA: Jossey-Bass Publishers.

Learning Forward. (2011). *Standards for professional learning.* Retrieved from http://www.learningforward.org/standards/index.cfm.

Levin, D. & Arafeh, S. (2008). *The digital disconnect: The widening gap between Internet savvy students and their schools.* Pew Internet and American Life Project by the American Institute for Research. Retrieved from http://www.pewinternet.org/

Maurer, M., & Davidson, G. (1998). *Leadership in instructional technology.* Upper Saddle River, NJ: Prentice Hall.

Meltzer, S., (2006). *An analysis of professional development in technology for elementary school teachers.* Dissertation Abstracts International, Section A, 67(06), 2119.

Meltzer, S. T. (2009). *Professional development in technology: An analysis of effective practices,* Paper presented at the meeting of Society for Information Technology & Teacher Education International Conference, Charleston, SC.

Merriam, S,. & Caffarella, R. (1999). *Learning in adulthood.* San Francisco, CA: Jossey-Bass Publishers.

National Center for Educational Statistics. (2009). *Digest of Educational Statistics, 2009.* Retrieved from http://nces.ed.gov/programs/digest/d09/

National Staff Development Council. (2009). *Status of professional learning.* Retrieved from http://www.learningforward.org/stateproflearning.cfm.

Partnership for 21st Century Skills (2009). *Framework for 21st century learning.* Retrieved from http://www.p21.org/documents/P21_Framework.pdf.

Roy, P. (2010). *Using the SAI to build a district professional development plan.* National Staff Development Council in collaboration with Arizona Department of Education.

U.S. Department of Education. (2010). *Transforming American education learning powered by technology: National education technology plan 2010.* Retrieved from http://www.ed.gov/technology/netp-2010.

Resources

Professional and Government Organizations

Association for Supervision and Curriculum Development (ASCD)—http://ascd.org/

International Society for Technology in Education (ISTE)—http://www.iste.org/welcome.aspx

National Center for Technology Planning—http://www.nctp.com/

National Education Association (NEA)—www.nea.org

National Staff Development Council (NSDC)—http://www.learningforward.org/index.cfm

Partnership for 21st Century Skills (2010)—http://www.p21.org/index.php

U.S. Department of Education
- ◆ www.ed.gov
- ◆ National Education Technology Plan 2010—http://www.ed.gov/technology/netp-2010

Hardware and Software Resources

The following resources are not meant as an endorsement but rather as a starting point as you begin researching the best solutions for your specific needs. Vendors and Web sites change constantly, so amend this list and add your own as you go.

Hardware Resources

Epson Projection Systems—http://www.epson.com/cgi-bin/Store/jsp/EdProjectors/Home.do

Interactive whiteboards (Many are on the market, including these.)
Smart Technologies—http://www.smartboards.com/
Promethean—http://www.prometheanworld.com/

Sony Projection Systems—http://pro.sony.com/bbsc/ssr/mkt-education/

Software Resources
Brainchild—www.brainchild.com
Compass Learning Inc.—www.compasslearning.com
Earobics—www.earobics.com
Inspiration—www.inspiration.com
Houghton Mifflin Harcourt—www.hmhinnovation.com
McGraw Hill Education—www.mhschool.com
Pearson Learning—www.pearsonschool.com
Scholastic Inc.—www.scholastic.com
Tom Snyder—www.tomsnyder.com

Appendix B:
Worksheets/Templates/Guides

- Pre-Planning Worksheet (Chapter 3)
- Needs Assessment Survey (Chapter 3)
- Technology Plan Guide (Chapter 4)
- Technology Inventory (Chapter 4)
- Long-Term Technology Plan Template (Chapter 4)
- Short-Term Technology Plan Template (Chapter 4)
- Training Schedule Overview (Chapter 5)
- Training Schedule A Template (Chapter 5)
- Training Schedule B Template (Chapter 5)
- Follow-Up Needs Assessment Survey (Chapter 6)

Pre-Planning Worksheet (Wish List)

I.   Goals (List all possible goals regardless of their priority.):

II. Learning community:
     A. Existing learning groups/teams:

     B. Additional learning groups/teams needed (These may overlap and may include others outside the community):

III. Options for meeting/training locations:

IV.   Options for meeting/training times:

V.   Training materials (wish list):

VI.   Resources (wish list):

VII.   Assessment/evaluation:

Needs Assessment Survey (Professional Development)

Consider the information needed to create a quality professional development plan. Faculty and staff must be able to develop a comfort level with the necessary hardware, software, and implementation plan in order to successfully meet the expectation level set for the goals. Modify this needs assessment survey by including questions that will provide appropriate and adequate information needed to create a plan.

Please respond to each question using the following scale:

1 = very uncomfortable, 2 = somewhat uncomfortable,
3 = somewhat comfortable, 4 = very comfortable

1. My comfort level using the following hardware:
   a. Computer ① ② ③ ④
   b. Projector ① ② ③ ④
   c. Interactive whiteboard ① ② ③ ④
   d. Digital camera ① ② ③ ④
   e. Other _____
2. My comfort level using the following type of software:
   a. Word processing ① ② ③ ④
   b. Desktop publishing (i.e. Microsoft Publisher) ① ② ③ ④
   c. Spreadsheet software (i.e. Excel) ① ② ③ ④
   d. Other _____
3. My comfort level using the hardware and/or software integrated into my lesson plans: ① ② ③ ④

Please answer the following questions by selecting YES or NO:

5. I would like to improve my comfort level using the hardware by:
   a. Attending appropriate scheduled training (initial, advanced, etc.) Ⓨ Ⓝ
   b. Receiving a manual or handouts Ⓨ Ⓝ
   c. Observing someone using the hardware Ⓨ Ⓝ
   d. Going to a Web site with training/support information Ⓨ Ⓝ
   e. Other (please describe your preference if not listed) _____
6. I would like to improve my comfort level using the software by:
   a. Attending appropriate scheduled training (initial, advanced, etc.) Ⓨ Ⓝ
   b. Receiving a manual or handouts Ⓨ Ⓝ
   c. Observing someone using the hardware Ⓨ Ⓝ
   d. Going to a Web site with training/support information Ⓨ Ⓝ
   e. Other (please describe your preference if not listed) _____

7. I would like to improve my ability to integrate the software into my lesson plans by:
    a. Attending appropriate scheduled training (initial, advanced, etc.) (Y) (N)
    b. Receiving a manual or handouts (Y) (N)
    c. Observing someone using the hardware (Y) (N)
    d. Going to a Web site with training/support information (Y) (N)
    e. Other (please describe your preference if not listed) _____
8. I would be willing to:
    a. Share my knowledge with other faculty/staff (Y) (N)
    b. Model the software/hardware/lessons in my classroom (Y) (N)
    c. Assist with training as a peer or team member (Y) (N)
    d. Develop training materials to support colleagues (Y) (N)
    e. Other: _____
9. The most important things in my opinion to consider when planning professional development are (#1 is the most important):

    1. _____

    2. _____

    3. _____
10. In my opinion, the goal of the professional development should be:

    _____

    _____

Technology Plan Guide

This guide is designed to help you gather and compile information to support the development of a short-term and a long-term technology plan. The following areas should be discussed and shared with any stakeholders. The compiled information should include:

I. **Goals/visions**
   A. Using the needs assessment survey or similar instrument, collect information focusing on the professional development needs and/or the infrastructure needs of:
      1. Faculty/staff status
         a. Beginning level
         b. Intermediate level
         c. Advanced/support level
      2. Infrastructure status—software, hardware
      3. Training needs based on status and project expectations (goals)
      4. Infrastructure needs based on project expectations (goals)
   B. Define a collaborative goal/vision for your technology plan. Develop a clear focus and be sure of the following:
      1. Be specific and clear when writing your goals.
      2. Be realistic and divide your goals into short-term and long-term in order to accomplish them in a realistic time frame.
      3. Make your goals measurable so progress and success can be determined.
      4. Consider roadblocks such as policies, funds, etc. to make sure goals are attainable.

II. **Actions**
   A. List all activities, and categorize them based on professional development, purchases, or installation. (Be specific based on your goals.)
   B. Reorganize activities sequentially in each category. Some may overlap and be ongoing. Identify these as such.
   C. Determine if actions can be divided into short-term or long-term actions. Some actions may reoccur in a long-term plan.
   D. These actions may be revisited at any time. It is better to include all activities and adjust them as the plan is redefined.

III. **Resources**
   A. Determine all resources that are available or needed. Consider human resources (support) as well as materials.
   B. When considering costs, indicate possible and realistic sources for funds.
   C. When considering human resources, indicate roles and responsibilities
   D. Review actions and make sure all actions have resources aligned to them.
   E. Consider incentives for professional development as resources needed. These do not necessarily need to be monetary in nature, but they may need approval or human resource support.

IV. **Evaluation**
   A. Define how the success of the goals will be measured and what method will be used to determine the level of success.
   B. Indicate a timeline for evaluation, and set realistic dates. Identify the purpose and what information may be determined for each evaluation.
   C. Consider a midproject evaluation to provide insight as to whether goals need to be adjusted, additional resources need to be provided, human resources need to be realigned, etc.
   D. Depending on the goal of your project, consider evaluation from students as well as from faculty and staff. This can often provide additional perspectives and resources not previously considered.

Technology Inventory

It is important during planning to have a complete inventory of all the relevant hardware, software, and other resources that are available. Many of these resources may be listed on previously completed inventories. However, the older inventories may not be complete or current. "Support" includes repair or missing parts that are needed such as cords or ink for printers. The following should be completed with the project goals and implementation plan in mind. Customize this table to meet the criteria of your plan.

I.   Hardware

Hardware	Number Available	Location	Responsible Person/Dept.	Support Needed?
1.				
2.				
3.				

II.   Software

Software	License/Access Available	Location	Responsible Person/Dept.	Support Needed?
1.				
2.				
3.				

Long-Term Technology Plan Template

Identify goals and activities that closely align to the school improvement plan or other district initiative. These goals should be long-term (more than one year). Depending on your alignment of goals, it may be better to use a spreadsheet for the responses for I, II, and III.

I.   School goal(s):

II.   Above goal(s) aligned to (school improvement plan, district initiative, grant, etc.):

III. Assessment/evaluation method/data (quantitative and measurable):

IV.   Sequential short-term technology plans/activities:

Goal	Activity Overview	Date	Location	Participants	Coordinator/ Responsible Person

Short-Term Technology Plan Template

This Short-Term Technology Plan should be focused and very specific. Modify the type of training and goals based on your own individual focus.

I.   Needs assessment data (from Needs Assessment Survey)
    A. Infrastructure needs
        1. Equipment (computers, printers, projectors, etc.)
        2. Software
        3. Services/support (installation, etc.)
    B. Professional development
        1. Faculty/staff needing professional development

Training (examples)	Faculty/Staff Number	Position
Beginning		
Intermediate		
Advanced		
Software		
Hardware		

II.   Goals/vision
    A. Overall long-term goal

    B. Short-term (one year or less) goal(s) (One or two of these should be selected from the Long-Term Technology Plan)

    C. Student impact expectation

    D. Faculty/staff impact expectation

III.   Action plan (List *all* activities sequentially.) (Year 1 plan)

Action/Activity	Date Beginning	Date Ending	Participants	Responsible Person(s)

IV.   Resources (List *all* resources needed to accomplish the short-term goal.)

Resource Needed	Source	Funding Needed	Funding Source	Responsible Party/ Person(s)
1.				
2.				
3.				
4.				

V.   Evaluation (Each goal or activity indicated in section III should be addressed in this section.)

Goals/Activities	Action Needed	Measurement Method	Documentation Needed	Date of Evaluation
1.				
2.				
3.				
4.				

Training Schedule Overview

Complete the following table by listing all trainings or professional development activities. Larger school districts may add additional similar tables for groups of trainings addressing specific district technology plans.

Targeted Goal _____

Expected Outcome _____

Measureable Assessment _____

Time Line: Begin _____   Complete _____

Date	Time	Location	Content	Expected Participants	Coordinator/ Trainer/ Responsible Person

Training Schedule A Template

Training times of one- or two-hour blocks for focused training and/or support may be scheduled throughout the day. Use this format to develop a training schedule. These training times may be:

☐ before school
☐ after school
☐ planning times (specific grade levels or subject areas with common planning)
☐ lunch period (participants bring their own lunch)
☐ teacher planning or work days
☐ other

In order to identify available options for training, complete the following table by blocking available training times for specific groups. Customize the columns based on times teachers are willing to train (early or late) or on class period times. The grade or subject areas in the first column should be customized based on the target audience to be trained. The results of this table will indicate whether it's possible to have training/collaborative groups meet together based on grade levels or subject areas.

Grade/Group	7:00	8:00	9:00	10:00	11:00	12:00	1:00	2:00	3:00	4:00
Kindergarten										
First										
Second										
Third										
Fourth										
Fifth										

Training Schedule B Template

This schedule provides a very cost-effective way to use substitute dollars for professional development. In this simple sample of a school training, four substitutes enable twelve teachers to participate in two-hour training blocks. The times may be adjusted by five to ten minutes on each side to account for movement between groups.

Begin with a blank schedule and customize columns by indicating the appropriate school times, blocks, or periods. The first column should be customized with individual teacher names. Include planning periods on the schedule to help stretch substitute time. It may be possible to cover another teacher's classroom when planning periods are taken into account. Classroom teachers and substitute teachers should eat lunch with their classes if possible; however, a lunch block is included for the coordinator/trainer. It may be necessary to build in a thirty-minute block before or after a training block to allow for lunch.

This simple schedule can be used as a framework. An after-school training for everyone can be included for follow-up, or an additional two-hour block can be added to train another group of teachers.

Teacher	8:00	9:00	10:00	11:00	12:00	1:00	2:00	3:00	4:00
A									
B									
C									
D									
E									
F									
G									
H									
I									
J									
K									
L									
Coordinator									

Follow-Up Needs Assessment Survey

In order to determine the progress and success of the professional development and technology plans, it is important for all participants to respond to questions regarding their perception of their learning environment and future needs. These results will be helpful in the revision of the plan and in meeting future needs so the faculty can achieve their goal(s).

I have attended the following number of scheduled technology workshops this school year:

_____ 0 workshops

_____ 1 workshop

_____ 2–3 workshops

_____ 4 or more workshops (please indicate how many: _____)

Please respond to the following questions using the following scale:

1 = very uncomfortable, 2 = somewhat uncomfortable,
3 = somewhat comfortable, 4 = very comfortable

1. My comfort level using the new hardware (ex: interactive whiteboard) is: ① ② ③ ④
2. My comfort level using the new software (ex: PowerPoint) is: ① ② ③ ④
3. My comfort level integrating the new technology into my lesson plans is: ① ② ③ ④

Please respond to the following questions using the scale:

1 = never, 2 = seldom, 3 = sometimes, 4 = frequently, 5 = always

4. I believe the principal is involved and committed to providing opportunities and support for this project. ① ② ③ ④ ⑤
5. Fellow teachers, trainers, and/or support consultants are available for help when I need it. ① ② ③ ④ ⑤
6. Opportunities are provided to observe other teachers modeling the new expected skill in the classroom. ① ② ③ ④ ⑤
7. Materials and resources are available when I need them. ① ② ③ ④ ⑤
8. The goals and expectation of the project are clear. ① ② ③ ④ ⑤

Please respond to the following questions:

9. The most valuable aspects/activities of this project for me have been:

_____

_____

10. In order to further develop my skills, I still need:

_____

_____